D1248775

Advance Praise

"With *When Grief Is Good*, Cindy Finch invites readers to consider looking at grief through a new lens. Processing grief is different for everyone; however, the impact it can have on relationships and health is universal. Cindy's professional wisdom and commitment to help people is evident in the pages of this book. She cuts through the noise and brings a voice of comfort and reality for understanding grief. This book is groundbreaking and a must-read for anyone looking to understand and process their losses."

—LORI JEAN GLASS,
AUTHOR AND FOUNDER OF PIVOT AND THE GLASS HOUSE

"Cindy's sage advice and wisdom come from her own painful journey of healing from childhood trauma and surviving cancer. This book is a must-read for anyone who has survived trauma and wants to transform that pain before it wrecks their relationships."

—CHRISTOPHER L. KREEGER, ESQ.

"Inviting Cindy Finch into your orbit is a bountiful choice. Her words will provide the foundation you've been searching for, as well as a safe place to return to when you need them. She'll sit in the gutter with you and help you climb out when you're ready."

—KAYLA REDIG, FILMMAKER OF VINCIBLE

"Cindy's formulation of meaningful pathways to navigate grief is authentic, insightful, practical, and clinically sound. This book is a must-read for anyone who is grieving."

—BRENT MOOS, LCSW, CLINICAL HOSPICE SOCIAL WORKER

"Throughout her own personal experiences of divorce, cancer, significant losses, and heartache, Cindy has asked the hard questions, cried, doubted, and risen strong to find good and joy on the other side. If you long to find purpose beyond your pitfalls, read this book."

—KELLY KARR, RN, MBA

"While it is not possible to feel happy all the time, When Grief Is Good will help you journey through loss, teaching you some ways to learn and grow while seeing yourself not as a helpless passenger but as a brave explorer of your own pain."

—KAREN LAWLER, PROFESSOR

"Cindy Finch has given us a gift of learning how to work through grief and to come out the other side healthier and stronger. There are few books that help us to really navigate the grieving process, and this is one of them! So grate-

ful that Cindy has taken her wisdom and expertise and shared it with the world! A definite must-read for anyone struggling with grief and loss."

—JENNIFER PLISKO, LCSW, THERAPIST

"Seen through the lens of her varied experience as a therapist and coach, along with her own journey through cancer and life-threatening illness, Cindy brings a unique perspective on grief—a perspective that is sure to bring healing and hope for a fulfilling life after trauma and loss. Essential reading for those navigating life after loss."

—SANDRA SCHOOLER, MINISTRY LEADER

"It's common to feel overwhelmed by a loss and feel confused about how to move forward. In this wonderful and needed book, Cindy Finch openly shares her deep wisdom about loss and grief and offers practical steps that guide readers along their own personal healing journey. You will feel understood and uplifted as you read this book."

—KATHY PURDY, LMFT, FAMILY THERAPIST

"The author brings her own real-life experiences to life. She makes you know you are not alone in your grief. She writes from the heart and her desire is for everyone who experiences grief and sadness in life (which is all of us) to know that there is life out there, and happiness can be achieved by working through the things on your journey that have brought you to this point. She brings you through your trials with laughter and love."

—KIM PATTERSON, HOSPITAL ALLIED STAFF

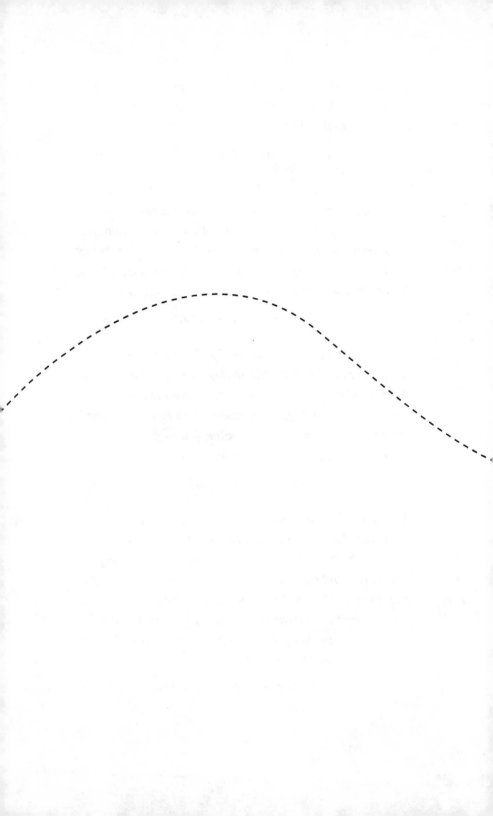

WHEN
GRIEF
IS
GOOD

TURNING YOUR GREATEST LOSS
INTO YOUR BIGGEST LESSON

Cindy Finch

LIONCREST
PUBLISHING

WHEN GRIEF IS GOOD

Turning Your Greatest Loss Into Your Biggest Lesson

ISBN   978-1-5445-2270-8   *Hardcover*
      978-1-5445-2268-5   *Paperback*
      978-1-5445-2269-2   *Ebook*
      978-1-5445-2392-7   *Audiobook*

For my "Four Favorites,"
Darin, Jordan, Zach, and Brandon.
I love you forever and I like you for always.

Contents

A Note on Faith

As a therapist and as a griever myself, I feel it's nearly impossible to separate matters of faith and spirituality from discussions about grief and loss. Grief and faith are such complex issues and so personal to every reader. Inevitably, when our world gets altered through loss, trauma, or unplanned events, there is an almost automatic questioning and curiosity, or anger and hostility about the idea of God.

Many people question God and believe that Somebody or Something should've been in control but was sleeping on the job when bad things happened. During times of suffering, even professed atheists, agnostics, or the most faithful devotees will often mull over questions about faith. There's something in the hearts of people going through this process of loss and disruption (in all its various forms) that clutches toward the spiritual. While you may read words in this book that refer to God, my request is that you fill in these words for yourself. While I use the word God, you may use a different word to express your faith. Everyone is at a different place on their path, especially in times of grief.

While this isn't a book about convincing you if God exists or not, it is a book about helping you understand your purpose in this world and where to go from here. Often as we ponder purpose, we also ponder meaning. The meaning of life, why we're here, where we came from, and what's next when this life is over. So it's only right that the spiritual is a part of our discussion.

Introduction

A t thirty-one, while pregnant, I found out I had cancer. A few years later, I went into heart, liver, and lung failure, and my doctors couldn't figure out why. I became disabled by the simultaneous failure of multiple organs, and I found myself in and out of several hospitals while trying to rebuild our lives after cancer. Our problems were compounded when one physician made a life-threatening mistake in my care. It was an accident, as they say, but it derailed my recovery, sent people with crash carts into my hospital room, landed me in another ICU, and added to a complex list of traumatic experiences familiar only to those who lose their health.

We finally found help out of state at the Mayo Clinic, where doctors performed open-heart and open-lung surgeries to save my life. In the wake of those surgeries, we moved our entire family from Nevada to Minnesota to be near the good healthcare at Mayo. As a result, my husband had to leave his job, and our three children had to leave behind their friends and grandparents and start new schools. We were a young family, both in our thirties, and uncertain how to handle this rapid-fire succession of hard things.

In the aftermath of those events, we needed some help to put things back together and move forward. Once settled, my husband Darin and I started going to couples therapy twice a week. We made our first appointment with a local therapist, Gary. We limped into his office, tired and worn out from our struggles. We shared an overview of all that had happened. Sitting across from us, even Gary began to cry.

Life had fallen hard on us, and our ability to cope could not keep up. In the presence of someone who could see and understand our off-the-charts stress, we began to heal. Gary would walk us down a road to recovery, using specific tools and training that would save our marriage, heal our minds, restore our struggling faith, and position us to help our children as well.

I would go on to heal many of my own childhood traumas and discover that contained within my loss and grief were the greatest clues to my life's mission: becoming a therapist. At the time, I didn't fully understand the significant loss we were experiencing, and that grief is a natural response to loss. The thing is, no one *wants* to walk through the barbed wire path of loss. I know I didn't. Grief is almost always synonymous with depression and sadness, and we do all we can to limit the time we spend wading through it. "Check, please!" Give me anything else; just make sure to get me out of my grief! And that's what we do—avoid grief.

We tend to manage the life losses we experience by feeling the initial hit and then quickly moving away from the event because it hurts. We will do anything to not sit in those heavy feelings for very long. We want to *move on, get over it, get back to work, feel normal again, just numb it*. We don't want to feel heavy emotions. In an attempt to quiet the pain of our grief, we work more, look at more screens, exercise more, eat more, drink more, watch more news or shows, and generally *avoid* the reality of the loss. But reality has a way of showing itself. All the feelings inside us do come out—more often than not, they come out sideways, through episodes of *emotional leakage*— outbursts, addiction, violence, suicidal urges, mental health problems, raging, or illness. Many of us lack an effective way to do the work needed within our loss and to move through our grief.

In her 1969 book *On Death and Dying,* psychiatrist Dr. Elisabeth Kübler-Ross introduced the traditional five stages of grief—denial, anger, bargaining, depression, and acceptance. These stages name our emotional states but do little to help us through them. The Big Five, as I like to call them, don't show people how to process and off-load their pain; they only show that grief exists in different forms. No one cares about forms or stages when their life has been gutted. When grief is left unprocessed or avoided, it can become debilitating and cause all sorts of problems, including, but not limited to, shame, the feeling of loss, making mistakes, shutting down, inability to focus, and more. It becomes *bad* grief. And if we're not careful, we get stuck in it until it just becomes who we are.

GRIEVING ON PURPOSE

Instead, I propose that we begin to see the work of managing our losses as a natural, even daily practice of intentional off-loading, like a pressure relief valve that gives our grief somewhere to go and a way to get there. I call this incremental process of off-loading *micro-grieving*, and it will stop the grief from building up, so it doesn't come out sideways. In short, when we grieve on purpose, a little at a time and make it normal, we can live better.

The breakthrough technique I use to treat the problem of grief overload and avoidance is a simplified but robust, invitation-based approach called the *Feel Better Framework*. Rather than using the Big Five to explain the stages of grief, which are a given, I show that the process of moving through loss and sorrow can be done as a series of small, specific activities and intentional practices. I explain how bite-sized pieces of time spent in certain ways can be effective to help shoulder the load of our loss, acknowledge our pain, and get back to a life worth living. People with all levels of loss can effectively move through their grief a little at a time so it doesn't become debilitating and lead to other problems.

Now more than ever, we need a way to think about grief and loss that fits our current-day value of efficiency and effectiveness. Even though grief may not be an efficient process, we can do it effectively.

---

*When we move through grief and learn all the lessons it is here to teach us, it can actually be quite **good** for us.*

When properly processed, our losses can become "good" grief. The relief and clarity many people experience on the other side of the grieving process can help them deepen into their own values, make needed changes in life, improve their sleep, energize their work, live with purpose, develop a sense of connection and gratitude, and so much more. Some experience enhanced focus and perspective, the ability to sort through and identify their priorities, illuminate a spiritual path, improve their character and their relationships, and even reveal a life's purpose. In my field, we refer to these sorts of changes as *post-traumatic growth*.

The Wildest Form of Love

Among our heavier states of being—like fear, anger, and shame—grief is not as clear and easy to see. For years, we've been taught that grief is what you go through when you lose someone or something important. And crying is a result of that loss. That's true. But that's not all.

Grief can be and feel like so many things. Megan Devine, author of *It's OK That You're Not OK*, calls grief *the wildest form of love*. The grieving have told me through my work as a licensed clinical social worker that sometimes it feels like they are numb automatons, moving through their day feeling *nothing*. Others have shared that their loss seems like a bomb has exploded across their whole family, shrapnel and debris everywhere. Still others say it's not so explosive but seems like there's a dark, hollow hole inside of them, and they are more like donut-people now, rather than solid forms. *Hollow* and *gaping* sit where *life* used to be before they experienced their loss. And others say it's a whole season, as if they are in a dark night of their soul for years at a time.

Others, myself included, can attest to all of these experiences and more. Many grievers who have walked through the swamplands of sorrow tell me they often have fits of rage and despair followed by times of extreme enlightenment and hope. As if the loss itself was meant to occur in order to clear them out and send them forward, galvanized and focused. Their loss brought relief; it brought clarity. The more they purged and clawed through their loss, the more it yielded the fruit of relief and direction.

Never before have we needed a systematic way to deal with grief like we do right now. *When Grief Is Good* is exactly that. This book guides you through difficult times and teaches you how to use severe loss as a springboard toward your next steps.

WHAT I KNOW ABOUT GRIEF

I have been a social worker for twenty-five years and have been helping people through grief as a therapist for more than a decade. Since completing a master's degree in Clinical Social Work and my training at Mayo Clinic, I've developed specialties in parenting today's teens and young adults, post-trauma growth, Dialectical Behavioral Therapy (DBT), complex-high-need-family interventions, traumatic loss and grief work for sudden death, and the management of life-altering illness. I am a clinical DBT family therapist and coach.

I've spent thousands of hours parenting, helping others, sitting with them after a layoff, in the middle of a divorce or new motherhood, or after the death of their child. I've met with grieving families in their homes, in the hospital, or in my office immediately following the death of a loved one. In my work as a California-based therapist, professor, and leadership coach, I pass forward specific tools and wisdom to help others find their way through hard times and keep a mindset of hope while they take their next steps.

Since 2013, I have authored and published works which

appeared on national websites and in publications like the *LA Times, St. Anthony's Press, HuffPost, Coping Magazine, Chasing the Cure, Rochester Women's Magazine,* and more.

Because I believe I can only take my clients as far as I've gone myself, I have stayed active in my personal growth and discovery since those early days with Gary. What I came to learn was that everything great I have ever done in my life has started with some type of loss. Much to my surprise, I found that grief can be *good for us.* If you let it, grief will change your life—whether that change is paralyzing or transformational is up to you.

By the end of this book, my hope is that grief won't carry so much shame for you. I hope you discover that avoiding or getting stuck in your grief is not the answer. And most of all, I want you to see that you have important work to do in this world. We'll begin in Chapter 1 by clearly identifying the grief. Grief is the best guru ever. It could launch you into a fulfilling career, a relationship, or the life of your dreams. If you let it, grief will change your life for the better.

The Slippery Slope:
Grief Avoidance

"Grief is work, avoiding grief is even more work."

—DAVID KESSLER

At one of our early therapy sessions with Gary, I reflected on a particularly traumatic phase of our journey. Sitting on the couch with my husband Darin, I remarked how lost and lonely I felt through the process of my illness, especially before I was properly diagnosed. When it was Darin's turn, he recounted his part of the experience and said, "Well, actually, that was when I stopped loving you."

When he said that, I froze. "Wait, what? You stopped *loving* me?" He went on to explain that so many things had gone from bad to worse in our lives and that he felt so overwhelmed that the only thing he could do was to stay dutiful as a husband and provider on the outside by driving me to appointments, caring for our kids, and paying the medical bills, but he couldn't stay emotionally connected to someone whose life was a sinkhole. Out of self-preservation, he had to disconnect from me. And I had felt it. There had been a wall between us for months as we moved through the duties of our tragedy but lacked the emotional, spiritual, and physical connections we had previously enjoyed. He was ducking for cover, and I couldn't blame him.

I had never gone through the slow, painful near loss of a spouse like he had. "Cindy, you were going to die, and you were the love of my life," he said. "How could I get closer and closer to you, watch you suffer, and then *also* prepare to lose you?" It was an impossible situation.

I sat stunned, hearing that my husband, my favorite person in the world, the man who had given me such great care for the last several years, who loved our kids and watched over all the details of their lives, had lost *all love* for me. I had felt it, but to actually hear him say it stung my soul. I was speechless. I didn't understand how anyone who loved me as much as he had could move farther away from me when I needed him most. I was dumbfounded by his confession. *Really*? He didn't *love* me anymore?

My sickness had the opposite effect on me. When faced with a life-threatening illness, I felt more love and connection to those around me than ever before. I experienced a greater love for and devotion to Darin during that time than at any other time in our lives. How could he have felt so differently?

After hearing his words, I sat silent in the counseling room. Down in the depths of me, a hot rage began to rise. Filling up with anger like a water balloon on a hose, my thoughts burned with accusations and heat. "Who stops loving someone who's sick and dying? What a terribly insensitive, hurtful thing to do!" I was furious.

Under Gary's careful watch, I looked at Darin and coldly asked, "Well, did you ever *start* loving me again, or is this it? Apparently, I've been such a burden to you that now you're done with me? We made it through all that, and now you're leaving?"

We didn't understand back then the toll that hard times could take on a marriage. We weren't aware that for caregivers like Darin, each and every treatment, surgery, or near-death episode, every debilitating condition that impacted me, *also* impacted him. The difference was that doctors would prescribe me medications, friends and family would cheer me on, and nurses would hold my hand when things were the toughest. But for caregivers like Darin, there were only more hospital bills, constant uncertainty, more traumatic news, and more pain. No direct support. Just loss and dismay at every turn. Of course he had withdrawn! Who among us could tolerate a full-frontal assault on their entire life and not flinch?

You see, we had no way to navigate our grief without the help of someone who could guide and contain us as we healed. Not only was our individual well-being at stake but so was the very survival of our marriage. And if our marriage went down, so would our kids. They had already suffered the stress of having a mom in chronic crisis for the past few years, a cross-country move, new schools, and sleep and behavior problems. As a family, we were a wreck...and now this!

He paused, looked at me, and said, "I'm trying. That's why I'm here. I don't want to quit on us."

And with that statement, we were launched into some of the richest, most valuable parts of our healing journey as a couple. We had come into counseling like survivors of an apocalypse, crawling up out of our bunkers, and walking around in a stupor as we surveyed the carnage and destruction on the landscape of our lives. We had no idea what to do next or which direction we should take to deal with all our loss. But Gary knew. He became our guide through the dark night of our souls.

We didn't know then that we were both having an array of responses to the losses we had experienced. We now call them *grief responses*.

THE SUBMARINE OF DENIAL

Did you know that the original five stages of grief were developed to explain what the *dying* were experiencing as they faced their own death? It was never intended to explain the experience of the ones who are still alive. However, there is some truth to the five stages, not just when facing the end of our own lives, but for losses of all kinds.

In the Introduction, I wrote about Dr. Elisabeth Kübler-Ross's 1969 book *On Death and Dying*. In her book, she explains that the dying often experience, at first, a rejection of their own situation. They experience shock and denial: *This can't be happening to me.* Denial is a temporary condition which often marks the beginning of the grieving process, though many don't recognize it as such. *How can I be grieving and denying at the same time?* Denial is a powerful drug, one that keeps us safe and mostly sane while living in our world. If we lived a denial-free life, we would hardly be able to walk out our front door, let alone get in our car and drive down the freeway to work. If we had to think about it every day, the sheer reality of crime, accidents, and sudden illness would leave us crippled in a corner, unwilling to take any risks in life. Our brains do us a favor, shielding us from the torrid facts of life by burying deep in our quiet subconscious mind most of the information we read about and experience. The prefix "sub" means "below the surface." Like a submarine below the surface of water, our subconscious mind keeps our vulnerability below the surface of our awareness. It allows us just enough fear to plan for disaster and wear our seatbelts but not enough that we hide under the covers every day. Without denial, we'd all be toast.

THE KICKING COHORT: ANGER

Once denial gives way (and it usually does), reality hits. And reality often brings with it a kicking cohort called anger. Individuals in this stage may find themselves jolted, lashing out and placing blame, which makes them quite difficult to be around and care for. They're pissed off at life, illness, doctors, family members, drivers in other cars, neighbors walking their dogs— they're even mad at the weather or at themselves. This is often the stage where cancer patients and their families wear T-shirts that read *F*ck Cancer* or *Kicking Cancer's Ass*. Anger is good.

Often, when we have to fight through a difficult situation, we can rally and make it through some pretty tough stuff with the energy that anger brings.

Like gasoline in the tank, anger can help us get up and handle shit: harsh treatments, lack of sleep, multiple hospitalizations, low funds, tough conversations, or whatever else is thrown at us.

LET'S MAKE A DEAL:
BARGAINING

Later on, or sometimes right away, those facing their own demise may try cutting deals with a Higher Power or seek extreme cures to buy more time. They know they will die, but they just want to live long enough to do X or Y—see the birth of their first grandchild, go to the Senior Prom, or take that trip they've been dreaming of. Kübler-Ross calls this bargaining. But when God doesn't come through, and the new experimental treatment falls short or leaves them even sicker than before, they may fall off the cliff of despair and into the next stage, which she identifies as Depression.

LOST IN THE WILDERNESS:
DEPRESSION

This stage, when the individual withdraws, falls silent, begins to cry, or refuses visitors, is the one we *typically* think of as grief. This is where the most apparent grieving happens. This is also the stage where grievers (both the dying and the surviving) have very little energy, feel like they're moving through mud, and can become detached and hopeless. We often see the *Three Ds* show up together: Depression, Discouragement, and Despair. Grievers can sometimes feel like the Three Ds are circling them like wolves ready for the kill, and they are helpless to resist. This is also where shame, a feeling of loss, making mistakes, or the sense of being a burden can emerge.

ZIPPER MERGE: ACCEPTANCE

But Kübler-Ross asserts there's one more stage ahead: acceptance. In this final stop on the journey, the individual begins to come to grips with his or her plight and moves into yielding to reality. Like a zipper merge on the freeway, the griever slides into a new lane that often feels more peaceful as they echo toward more resolution than revolution. From those in acceptance, we often hear phrases such as "It is what it is" or "God has a plan" or "I want to enjoy what time I have left." According to Kübler-Ross, if the dying person reaches this phase, they have important work to do to prepare themselves and their loved ones (physically, emotionally, spiritually) for the actual process of death.

The Kübler-Ross model is recognized worldwide as a solid framework for those experiencing loss. Although she first identified the five stages as the emotions experienced by those *dying* from a terminal illness, eventually, she reworked the model so that it applied to more general loss as well (death of a loved one, or loss of a job, income, or freedom). She also later recognized that people could move in and out of the stages and that there was not a linear procession. In her book *On Grief and Grieving* (2004), feeling for *herself* the agony of facing death, a dying Kübler-Ross said to her coauthor David Kessler, "People love my stages, they just don't want to be in one."

WHY THE BIG FIVE DON'T HELP

The Big Five have held their own through the years. Whether we are dying, losing someone, experiencing job loss, divorce, or the end of a relationship, or any of the myriad experiences of loss that make up the human condition, the Big Five of loss hold true. But why isn't it more mainstream?

Though the Kübler-Ross model is well known by those in the medical and mental health professions, it is only mildly understood by the general populous. Unless you've placed a loved one on hospice and been given the little blue booklet *Gone from My Sight: The Dying Experience*, by nurse Barbara Karnes, then you are likely not well educated on loss. And here's why: When we hear the details of the voyage called grief, and we see that the itinerary includes things like denial, anger, bargaining, depression, and acceptance, we don't want to go. And when we begin to feel all the feelings of the Big Five, we'd rather do anything than experience the hot, dangerous, confusing sensations they bring.

I suspect that the rather brilliant naming of the stages of grief holds less interest for those in mainstream society mostly because *no one cares* about specific language when the shit hits the fan. For instance, how pertinent would any of this information have been to my husband and me in those early days of therapy?

The Big Five are technically correct, but they're not really humane. Aside from using them like road signs (which is important), they only belong in a small part of the average person's vocabulary. They are *an overview* and maybe even an *explanation* for what happens in the process of losing someone or something that was very important to us. But they don't teach us how to *go through* that loss. Like taking your driver's test at the DMV, you may have studied the traffic laws and practiced with your parents, but that can't do much to help you when you're behind the wheel of a car on a freeway at eighty miles per hour while other cars are whizzing around you, brake lights are flashing ahead, a police siren is coming up from behind, and it's starting to rain. Driver's training manuals and driving schools, like grief language, don't mean a damn thing when life is hard. What we need is a *way* to know we are moving through and doing the work of our grief, and then we need hope for what comes next.

HOW WE DEAL WITH GRIEF AS A SOCIETY

Another problem unaddressed by the Big Five is how we deal with grief as a society. We don't have a good "grief IQ" when it comes to moving through our various losses. Families don't transmit the importance and value of grieving, so no one has taught us how to process grief. Grief just isn't a thing we teach our kids, nor do we talk much about it in our culture. As a general rule, we value success, efficiency, health, and relevancy, but not grief.

Underneath addiction in its many iterations—alcoholism, drug addiction, workaholism, overeating and food addictions, retail therapy, irresponsible spending, or compulsive gambling—is a large well of grief that's been avoided. People don't want to look at it; they don't want to drop down to the emotion that lies beneath the surface. They constantly stay above it, trying to outrun it by drinking it away, using drugs, working a hundred hours a week, or overspending because if they truly feel it, they know it'll hurt.

Loss, though painful, can be a natural invitation to slow down and reflect. We miss that because our culture pushes us to produce.

A lot of people take time off for a funeral or take a few days before they search for another job, but rarely do we take the time to thoroughly understand and get under our loss. *What happened to me? What's going on? What are the messages for me? What did I miss?* Most often, we push through, push it aside, and get busy again.

The Old Way: Just Move On

When it comes to handling hard feelings like grief overload, here's what our present-day model would look like if it were a math equation:

Move + More + Avoid = Stuck

Recently, I spoke with a client who we'll call Kendra. She lost her brother Len when she was eight years old. Len was three years older, and she remembers him being the fun and funny one in the family. Always quick to make a silly face, give her a ride on his back like a horse, or talk in cartoon voices, Len was a goof in a family of stoics. She remembered his sly humor and comical presence as a bright light in her childhood. She shared a room with him for a period of time, and she and Len would stay up at night playing cards, looking at comic books, or secretly watching TV after lights out. Len was all the permission she needed to bend the rules; he was her partner in crime. *He was older, so it must be OK!*

One day, she came home from school to find the police in her kitchen and her parents at the kitchen table, her mom holding her head in her hands, sobbing. No one explained to

Kendra what was happening, but she could tell it wasn't good. They spoke about a bicycle, a train track, and an accident. The rest of the details are spotty, but the feeling in her chest, like a cement block, was what stood out. Before she ever heard that Len had "died," she had the feeling that he was gone. Nothing felt right. Something physical told her that the brother she loved, who had given her access to the lighthearted side of life, had suddenly been taken from her, and he was never coming back.

Eventually, her mom and dad would arrange for a small funeral where aunts and neighbors walked up sniffling and hugging her before quickly moving away like she had a contagious disease. They seemed to both feel sorry for her and want to get away from her as quickly as possible. "Len is no longer with us," was all they ever said to her. They never said what happened to him, who was to blame, where he went, what to do when you lose someone, or how to think about life in the wake of loss.

From that point on, Kendra saw her parents go through life in a numb, robotic way. They did what normal people did in life—went to work, made dinner, did chores—but a dark cloud encircled them. Never again did her mom or dad ever talk about her older brother. Kendra learned that to survive in a family who avoids hard topics, she would have to lock down her feelings. What felt familiar and safe to Kendra was to detach from her heavy emotions on the inside and get busy looking successful on the outside. Living separately from her feelings is what she knew because it's what her parents did when her brother died. Like Dr. James Dobson says, "More is caught than taught in families." What Kendra caught from her parents was how to avoid difficult losses and not talk about them. She was conditioned early to act not only as if nothing was wrong but also as if nothing had even happened. *Just move on.* The result? Pervasive anxiety, over-controlling behaviors, and a tendency to hide her emotions under layers of avoidant strategies meant to keep the inner parts of herself safe from more tragedy.

When Kendra got older, her attachment system—the interpersonal mechanism we use to bond with others in relationships—sought out the same type of attachment with adults that she had become accustomed to while growing up. Aloof and detached, Kendra met her world in a way that ensured she would win, at least on the outside. The friends and partners she chose were outwardly successful but consistently shallow, anxious, and emotionally cut off from the deeper parts of themselves and others. As an adult, Kendra partnered with a series of emotionally unavailable men that could not show up as healthy adults or hold a deeper, supportive presence with her. They did not understand or talk about their emotions or take responsibility for themselves outside of work and finances.

Even with her two teenagers, she tended to relate to them based on how they performed in school and in sports rather than from unconditional love and acceptance. She used a challenging, pressure-filled approach to parenting, telling herself they'd need someone to be hard on them if they were going to make it in the world. Not surprisingly, her kids kept many secrets from her and preferred spending time with their friends or at their dad's house. They showed her their grades and gold medals but not their hearts.

Rarely vulnerable and open, Kendra did what she had to do in life to survive. The eight-year-old child within longed to express her love, care, and missing of her brother but didn't know how to do this as an adult. No one ever showed her. She felt so alone and couldn't figure out why. How could she have so much financial security, outward success, and apparent competence, yet feel so lonely and lost in her relationships? She came into therapy complaining of migraine headaches, poor sleep, a sense of restlessness at work, and dissatisfaction in her love life (always anxious to find her knight in shining armor, only to have them all leave her). She had become quite good at Move + More + Avoid = Stuck.

The New Way: The *When Grief Is Good* Snapshot

Talk + Feel + Move = Relief

If Kendra had a healthy grief IQ, she would have been taught the following:

- How to grieve

- What grief feels and looks like in everyday words

- The importance of honoring and remembering her brother

- How to talk about and actually experience heavy emotions

- Ways to honor her brother

- The special gifts her brother had given her from his life

This is what I offer to myself and to my clients when they're in the deep end of their grief, a way to talk, feel, and move through their loss so they can experience relief. As they learn to purge the heavy mass of the loss inside them, they're often surprised to discover that all this grief, all the horrid parts of it, are *good* for them.

THE DOORWAY FOR GREAT CHANGE

I could relate with Kendra. That feeling you get when something awful is happening, the sensation when your throat constricts, and your center drops out. That's the feeling I had for most of my childhood. I came to grief much like everyone else. By the time I realized what it was, I was already on overload.

I remember my childhood and adolescence like this: a long series of strange, sometimes fun, often lonely, chaotic, and traumatic events that happened but were never spoken about. No one had ever shown me or opened up a dialogue with me about how to deal with hard things. I locked them inside until all that unprocessed grief started coming out of me through panic attacks. I had my first panic attack when I was eight or nine. What brought it on was listening to my brother and sister fight and hit each other. Sitting on the closed toilet seat in our tiny trailer, not knowing what to do or how to talk about it, my body took over, and I was flooded by the first of hundreds of panic attacks I'd have throughout my life. When I was sixteen, my best friend Celeste was killed in a car accident. I'm thankful to have been at her funeral, but we never talked about it after that. Dozens more life events (as they're called in my field), left unprocessed, lay just below the surface for the first twenty-nine years of my life.

A Decade of Epic Failure

When childhood was over, my siblings and I were like feral cats, darting out the barn doors when we turned eighteen. We left childhood behind, with absolutely no idea what had happened to us or how to even talk about it.

My two sisters and I eventually *talked about it* through our behaviors. All three of us got married at a young age and then haphazardly divorced from men who were poor matches for us. Our unprocessed childhood grief only came to light in our sequential relational failures.

At twenty-seven, I remember walking back to work from divorce court, nine months pregnant, in the rain, wondering if things could get any worse. By the time I was twenty-eight, I had two young kids, was on welfare, and had moved back to my parents' house to try and begin again. I felt like an epic failure.

By the time I met my second husband Darin, I had already been divorced, gone bankrupt, had my small house fore-closed, and had both cars repossessed. When I turned thir-ty-one, I got cancer. I would go on to survive cancer, and then heart, liver, and lung failure. And although I can't prove this, and I rarely talk about it, I've always wondered if the health problems of my thirties were a result of all the unprocessed problems of my childhood and my young adult years. If only

I'd had permission and a way to steadily off-load everything that had backed up inside of me all those years, perhaps my health would not have toppled the way it did. I wish someone would've taught *me* how to grieve.

TEACHING MYSELF HOW TO GRIEVE

The difference between the early losses of growing up and the losses of my later years was, of course, that I had a more adult brain with which to manage my loss. That's important. The other big thing is that I decided to run a different play with my life. I started talking. To everyone. About nearly everything. I made it my goal to leave no loss or struggle unspoken about ever again. And it helped. It especially helped after cancer. When Darin and I began seeing Gary, we were already primed to receive his help. It was a game changer over time.

I could see that when I faced into and spoke about a difficult experience (with someone safe and supportive), whatever it was, it seemed to lighten my load and help me manage my emotions, and it also gave me a little burst of hope. Then, I could more easily find my next steps. Once I wasn't roaming around feeling lost in the maze of sideways emotions, I was better able to find my next move. Whether the *next move* was to take a nap or find a new job, the point is, when I became intentional about grieving—feeling it, talking about it, moving through it—grief became a process for me of *getting clear* rather than one that *bogged me down*.

I also found that eventually, I didn't need a therapist or a leader to guide me through; I could be my own healer and create my own magic. After a loss, I began seeing my own sideways emotions as messages to myself—like text messages. *Hey, listen up!* Or if my sleep was off, my energy low, or my thoughts spinning—*Cindy, you have new messages in your inbox.* They became signals to attend to myself and my process of grieving. I could almost always link the heavy emotion (usually one of the Big Five) or other problems to the loss event itself. And then, once I understood a bit more about what was happening in me, I found a trusted person to talk to (coworker, friend, family member, roommate, partner, group member) for just a few minutes. Not spewing my deepest self, just a little release that sounded like "Yeah, I lost my best friend a few months ago. I came across a picture of us yesterday and it tore me up. Ugh. I felt 'off' the rest of the day." If they made eye contact with me, validated what I was experiencing (even a little), and let me share a bit of my struggle, that was enough. I felt better. I could go on for that time. Pressure relieved for now. In short, I *taught myself* how to grieve.

What did teaching myself how to grieve look like? Whatever it took. Small actions every day so I wouldn't be stuck in my grief. We can't bypass our loss, no matter how much we want to; we have to process our grief, take our difficulties and make them our friends. Loss feeds learning. We can either lean in or *check out*.

If no one was available for me to talk to, I wrote down what I was experiencing in whichever way worked for me: poetry, essay, story form, anything! If I couldn't do that, I prayed. If I didn't have much faith in my faith that day, I'd go online and look for others going through the same thing and read their thoughts or post my own. I would text a friend. I would find a song that fit my situation and sing it *out loud*. Just a little something, all the time, to make it through that moment, that day, that feeling.

Other times, I didn't feel the need to talk about it; I just needed to move and do something with it. One time, I wrote a thank-you letter to God and mailed it. In it, I detailed how grateful I was to get my health back and stay with my family a little longer. I'll never know where that letter ended up. Another time, I embarked on a little *pay-it-forward* exercise. I calculated exactly how many days I had been sick one year—it was 270. After I regained some energy, I committed an act of kindness every day for the next 270 days. That little action gave me the extra energy I needed to move myself through the grief and rebuilding phase of my survivorship.

OK. Wait. Stop. Hold on. Did you just read that all I ever did was grieve in tiny bits and pieces here and there, and that was it? Aw, geez, no. Not even close. Grief, true grief, would never stand for that. The Big Five have been the go-to definition of grieving because they are *big*. My experiences with denial, anger, blame, depression, and acceptance have been legendary. Huge. I have been thoroughly jacked up by all five of them more times than I care to write.

My *conversations* with grief, if you want to call them that, have been deep and fervent. Sitting with good leaders and counselors has helped tremendously. We even told our kids we might not have a huge college fund for them, but we definitely have a therapy fund with their name on it! Big Grief has thrown me down on the mat more times than I can write, but—and this is important—it has not sidelined me and stolen my life *ever again.* It can't. I'm onto it now. The way to eat the elephant of grief, as the saying goes, is not to avoid it but to chew that sucker up one little bite at a time.

In the next chapter, we'll take what I've learned to do for myself and apply it to your situation as a way to locate your grief.

Chapter 2

The Grief Response Checklist

"In the midst of winter, I found there was, within me, an invincible summer.

And that makes me happy. For it says that no matter how hard the world pushes against me, within me, there's something stronger—something better, pushing right back."

—ALBERT CAMUS

THERE AREN'T ENOUGH WORDS

On January 26, 2020, a helicopter departed from John Wayne Airport in Orange County, California with nine people aboard: Kobe Bryant, a well-loved professional basketball player; his thirteen-year-old daughter Gianna; six family friends; and the pilot. The group was traveling for a basketball game. Due to light rain and fog that morning, most other air traffic was grounded, and the helicopter turned south toward the mountains. You probably know the rest of this story. Forty-one minutes after takeoff, the helicopter crashed into the side of a mountain. Bryant, his daughter, and the other seven occupants were killed.

Vanessa Bryant, Kobe's wife of eighteen years, shared this message on her personal Instagram page in February 2020:

I've been reluctant to put my feelings into words. My brain refuses to accept that both Kobe and Gigi are gone. I can't process both at the same time. It's like I'm trying to process Kobe being gone but my body refuses to accept my Gigi will never come back to me. It feels wrong. Why should I be able to wake up another day when my baby girl isn't being able to have that opportunity?! I'm so mad. She had so much life to live. Then I realized I need to be strong and be here for my 3 daughters. Mad I'm not with Kobe and Gigi but thankful I'm here with Natalia, Bianka and Capri. I know what I'm feeling is normal. It's part of the grieving process. I just wanted to share in case there's anyone out there that's experienced a loss like this. God I wish they were here and this nightmare would be over. Praying for all the victims of this horrible tragedy. Please continue to pray for all. (Vanessa Bryant, widow)

I wanted to capture this story because Vanessa Bryant articulates her loss in a relatable way. In this double, very public tragedy, she has become an accidental leader, a voice where others experiencing loss can find themselves. Sharing publicly is the process of identifying her grief and beginning to move through it. She is in deep pain, yet she still must carry on with life. The dichotomy between finding herself in this grief—angry, shocked, hurt, and lost—while simultaneously having to put one foot in front of the other to take care of her children is relatable for anyone experiencing loss. Her willingness to share in such a public way gives others permission to experience their own grief.

LOCATING YOUR GRIEF

Before we can begin to address our grief, we must first understand that we are experiencing it, and know what it looks like. Grief often shows itself in a way that many people don't recognize. After a significant loss or disappointment, many of us seek to numb our feelings. The aching hole we feel in our chest or the shame we experience because of the betrayal seem altogether too much for us to bear, so we search for ways to *not* feel.

There are dozens of songs about tears in our beer, red wine and sedatives, heartbreaks drowned out by random hookups with strangers...all of this might seem like a normal response to deep pain. As humans, we want to move *away* from pain, not toward it. From a young age, we are taught to pull our hands away from things that hurt us, like a hot stove or a bee sting. Our knee-jerk response to pain is to run away. But with life losses, we may accidentally roll into ineffective choices in an attempt to numb out these feelings. And then we start thinking our *numbing behaviors* are the problem rather than the reasons we wanted to numb out in the first place.

For example, drinking heavily after a loss, getting DUIs, or getting fired from work are often grief responses we treat as addiction or poor work performance. It's not uncommon for people to exhibit addictive behaviors after a significant loss. Others become severely depressed or suicidal. Many just can't function and don't want to feel. But the urge to numb it out is a *side effect* of heavy loss.

We might also avoid going to the intersection where our loved one died; blame ourselves for what happened; have recurring thoughts like *If only I had done this*; obsessively replay the incident in our mind, as it was or with a different outcome; or ask *why. Why wasn't I there to comfort them? Why did this happen?* Being furious at God, losing faith. These are all side effects of grief.

People may also avoid grief by hyper-focusing on a detail related to the loss, such as a lawsuit. This might present as suing the city, prolonged divorce proceedings, or abusive litigation. While court proceedings after a significant loss are typical and may provide a sense of control and justice, they can become the focus rather than a by-product of the loss event. As a therapist, I have seen entire families crippled by lengthy and vicious court battles related to custody, spousal support, or visitation rights after a divorce. Hundreds of thousands of dollars are spent on lawyers while the couple stays in a kind of suspended animation of denial after the loss of their partnership. One or both of them stay locked into a refusal to accept that they've "lost" in the relationship or "lost" their power. With such a vicious drive toward payback, they end up derailing the well-being of their children and even enduring physical and mental illness when they should be bolstering themselves to move forward in their new life as divorced co-parents. They get stuck in their grief response of denial, anger, and blame and wind up paying a huge price.

These are extreme examples that illustrate how we can be so intent on making someone pay for our loss that we don't see it as our grief coming out sideways. What's actually at play is our denial, our anger, and our unwillingness to accept current circumstances.

Negative Life Events are Normal

Please note: when we experience such profound loss, it is not unusual to experience symptoms of clinical depression, develop anxiety or panic disorders, or even have a psychiatric emergency. When I worked in a hospital setting, the "cause for admission" noted on many patients' charts was a *negative life event*. Negative life events are all the things we've been discussing so far: job loss, divorce, betrayal, miscarriage, death of a loved one, the pandemic, being a victim of a crime, and more. These life events are powerful, dark punches to the gut of who we are. I have seen people end their lives over some of these life events because they are so difficult to endure. It's important to understand this because if you find yourself with dark thoughts, panic attacks, crippling depressive episodes, urges to end your life, or other mental health challenges, you'll want to take steps to keep yourself safe and get the care you need.

A TOOL TO BRING RELIEF

The Grief Response Checklist is the first tool for you to properly identify your grief: what happened, how did you react, and what emotions surround that circumstance?

It's important to understand exactly what grief is doing in you and what it feels like, so you can get your hands around it and not accidentally slide into years of avoidance and denial. Grief is so much more than just a few heavy feelings. When we lose someone or something we care about, our body and mind signal the loss in a number of ways. Our attachment systems (the emotions and actions that bond us to others) go into a state of shock and withdrawal, as author Lori-Jean Glass puts it. Like a drug addict coming off heroin, we experience a state of intense separation from the thing or person we lost, and it feels like we're unable to face forward and continue as we once were.

As we experience deep loss, we respond in so many different ways: some describe a sinking feeling or a hole in their chest; others go totally numb and withdraw; others may become enraged and violent. It's essential to understand that your particular grief response is normal, and you can work with it. Otherwise, you may fall down the slippery slope of grief avoidance and end up trying to outrun or numb these difficult feelings. With proper care, you can heal your grief and then move into the payoffs of working through your loss, honoring your loved one, and emerging better on the other side of your pain and disappointment. Now, review these typical responses to grief and check off all that apply to you. Most people don't realize how their loss is affecting them.

BEHAVIORS

- ☐ Avoiding places, people, or activities that hold reminders of my loss
- ☐ Lack of interest in affection and romance
- ☐ Desire or planning for retribution
- ☐ Difficulty with returning to work
- ☐ Feeling like there's an elephant in the room
- ☑ Fear of more bad things happening
- ☑ Forgetfulness
- ☐ Holding on to unachievable goals
- ☐ Inability to cry
- ☑ Inability to make decisions
- ☐ Inability to set the loss aside for a period of time
- ☐ Increased use of drugs and alcohol
- ☐ Just "surviving"
- ☐ Lack of a future outlook
- ☐ Lack of care or trust for other people
- ☐ Lack of hope

- ☐ Lack of inner peace or well-being
- ☑ Lack of interest in life
- ☐ Lack of self-care
- ☐ Lengthy/hopeless lawsuits
- ☐ Looking at pictures, listening to their voice, smelling their clothes, trying to recall what it was like to be together
- ☐ Needing to support and protect children
- ☐ Having to learn over and over again about your loss
- ☐ Not wanting to be social
- ☐ Self-blame
- ☐ Stalking, driving by accused perpetrator's home or family
- ☐ Strained relationships
- ☐ Time-sliding
- ☐ Urges to see, touch, hear or smell things to feel close to the person or thing you lost
- ☐ Worries about financial security
- ☐ Yearning for your loved one

THOUGHTS

- ☐ His/her death was my fault.
- ☐ His/her death was useless. What did he/she sacrifice his/her life for?
- ☐ I am a bad person for letting this happen.
- ☐ I am devastated. Since this happened life has no meaning. It is purposeless.
- ☐ I am suffocated by my anger.
- ☐ I am trapped.
- ☐ I asked God to help me (them), and He did not.
- ☐ I can never feel completely safe again.
- ☐ I continually dream about revenge.
- ☐ I didn't do anything right when he/she was alive.
- ☐ I feel cheated.
- ☐ I feel guilty about all of the unfinished business between us. I never got a chance to say I was sorry.
- ☒ I have trouble making sense of this.
- ☐ I haven't been able to put the pieces of my life together since this event.
- ☒ I keep asking *why* questions, but there are no satisfactory answers.
- ☐ I keep asking, "Why me? Why my child?"
- ☐ I killed him/her.
- ☐ I must suffer as he/she suffered.
- ☒ I never got a chance to say a proper goodbye.
- ☐ I repeatedly think about how things could have been different.

- ☐ I was betrayed.
- ☐ I was not there to comfort him/her when he/she died. He/She died alone.
- ☐ I was so busy and too self-absorbed that I overlooked (denied) the warning signs.
- ☐ It is not right to enjoy myself.
- ☐ It is too painful. I do not want to think about it.
- ☐ Life has nothing to offer me anymore.
- ☐ Since _____ happened, I feel worthless, directionless.
- ☐ This is God's punishment.
- ☐ This loss (death, divorce, tragedy) has robbed my life of meaning.
- ☐ Experiencing "If only" thoughts
- ☐ Hallucinations
- ☐ Now I am up against a wall.
- ☐ Influence of hindsight bias
- ☐ Intrusive thoughts and flashbacks
- ☒ Questioning "Why?"
- ☐ Repeatedly imagining loved one's plight at the time of death
- ☐ Repetitive thoughts about the loved one's suffering
- ☐ Replaying scenes from the death over and over
- ☐ Ruminations about your loved one
- ☐ Worrisome thoughts about the future

The Grief Response Checklist

PHYSICAL SYMPTOMS

- ☐ Aches and pains
- ☐ Anxious/low mood/ moving slow
- ☐ Bouts of crying
- ☐ Chest pain, "broken heart"
- ☐ Difficulty concentrating
- ☐ Feeling numb or dissociated
- ☐ Headaches/migraines
- ☐ Increased or decreased appetite
- ☐ Increased or irregular heartbeat

- ☐ Irritable/angry
- ☐ Lack of interest in sex or romance
- ☐ Lack of sleep or sleeping too much
- ☐ Physical weakness
- ☐ Sense of being empty
- ☐ Sense of insecurity
- ☐ Feeling like you're in "withdrawal"
- ☐ Feeling a hole in oneself

EMOTIONAL SYMPTOMS

- ☐ A feeling of extreme vulnerability
- ☒ A feeling of unreality
- ☐ A sense of being abandoned, empty
- ☒ Anxiety/fearfulness
- ☐ Bitterness
- ☐ Depression/despair
- ☐ Detachment
- ☐ Feeling as if a part of oneself has died that can never be regained
- ☐ Frustration
- ☐ Guilt

- ☐ Hopelessness
- ☐ Inconsolable emotional pain
- ☐ Irritability/anger
- ☐ Loneliness
- ☒ Being numb
- ☐ Overwhelm
- ☐ Powerlessness
- ☐ Regret
- ☐ Relief
- ☒ Sadness
- ☐ Shock

MYTHS OF GRIEF

- ☐ "I am a burden to others."
- ☐ "No one can help me, no one understands."
- ☐ "I have to do this on my own."
- ☐ "I should be stronger."
- ☐ "Listening to the stories of others who've gone through this will make me feel worse."
- ☐ "People are tired of hearing about my loss."
- ☐ "This is just how it is."
- ☐ "I am dishonoring the deceased by getting better."
- ☐ "I am leaving him/her behind."
- ☐ "Feeling happier means that he/she is no longer important to me."
- ☐ "My love for him/her is fading."
- ☐ "Other people are comparing their grief to mine and theirs is worse."

SPIRITUAL SYMPTOMS OF GRIEF

- ☒ Anger at God
- ☐ Avoidance of religious settings
- ☐ Cynicism towards those of faith
- ☐ Doubts about one's faith, God, goodness
- ☐ Fear and ruminations about loved one's plight in eternity
- ☐ Feeling as if one is in *a dark night of the soul*
- ☐ Loss of spiritual direction
- ☒ An ongoing search for meaning
- ☒ Questioning God's plan
- ☒ Questioning one's faith
- ☐ Second-guessing beliefs and promises once held dear

This Grief Response Checklist can bring relief in the following ways:

- By looking at the list, you learn that your feelings are normal and "fit" somewhere. If it's on the list, others have felt it too, so you are not alone. This can help you feel more hopeful.

- You look at the checklist and find words and phrases for what's been happening to you that you didn't even realize was occurring. Now, with the definitions laid out in front of you, you can see that it's a normal grief response and that there is nothing wrong with you.

- You can begin to increase compassion for yourself and give yourself a break. You may even move away from shame and guilt when you start to work on the true story of your sadness, which is your story of loss.

This chapter is an invitation to locate yourself on a checklist of typical behaviors, thoughts, physical sensations, emotional responses, spiritual experiences, and myths that most of us experience in the face of loss.

The Story

The second tool of the Grief Response Checklist is called The Story, and it's where you get to write *your* story. I invite you to answer specific and short prompts about your story of loss. The Story can help define what has happened to you. And in a later chapter, you can use it as an internal scaffolding from which to work.

Grief is complex and multifaceted. For example, one of the most common problems with grief is difficulty sleeping. In the midst of grief, people often feel a sense of chaos and uncertainty about the event itself, and it keeps them up at night. Some clients experience insomnia because the parts and pieces of their loss swirl in their heads like ruminating thoughts, preventing the occurrence of good sleep. And if they do fall asleep, they may have fitful dreams and disturbing nightmares as their subconscious minds try to sort through what's happened. The purpose of getting your grief story down on paper is to keep it from swirling in your head so much and give it somewhere to go.

Whether you're experiencing insomnia or a different grief response, The Story assignment helps you consolidate your experience. Getting it out of your head, putting some rules or parentheses around it, and creating separation between yourself and these thoughts creates an opportunity to safely look at what's happening. For instance, if you notice you're irritable, short-tempered, impatient, or harsh with others after your loss, this exercise can help you understand *why* you feel so angry. It will help move the feelings out of your head and onto a piece of paper with some order and sequence, so you can stand back and look at your emotions and feelings rather than just be in them.

This exercise provides a way to look at what happened, articulate how your life has changed, and address what needs to happen next.

In short, you can process the anger resulting from your loss rather than just live in it. The anger part of your grief, though normal, can be better managed and healed by learning to move through, digest, understand, and process the obsessive or upsetting thoughts that keep you up at night. At the very least, you can consolidate them, allowing for a bit more rest.

This isn't a part with a silver lining. Right now, we're surveying the landscape. This is part of acknowledging your grief. We are just identifying here. There's nothing to do but to get clarity about your loss, so you know you experienced it. For instance, Kendra, whom I mentioned in Chapter 1, identified migraines and problems with her intimate relationships as the reasons to start counseling. She also had sleep problems. After thoroughly discussing her relationship issues and completing a few assignments around them, she still noted sleep problems, until one day, we spent an extended session talking about her brother. It was his birthday, and she felt a pang of sadness when she woke up that day. Thinking it was important to talk about it, she came to our meeting with some memories of their childhood, and we wound up spending a full hour talking about his life and what she recalled about losing him. The next day, she called to say that after our meeting, she went home and cried heavily for a long time about her brother, and for the first time in a long time, she slept through the entire night and woke up feeling refreshed and lighter. Expressing her grief through conversation and natural emotions was so very good for her.

Your Story

The prompts below are a formalized version of the framework I've used over and over again, in my own stories of loss and when I work with the grief-stricken. They are the things I'd say to myself or hear repeatedly, such as *I wish I had a time machine because I would do or say things differently.* Or *I didn't realize how much that person did for me.* Or *I didn't realize that I reacted by going numb.* This exercise helps you stand back from your story, look at it from the outside, and provide a little objectivity to put the pieces of it together. I developed these prompts so you can get a hold of your grief and speak to your-self and to others about your loss.

These prompts can be written or spoken. You don't have to write every single answer or think through every one; just pick the ones that make sense for you.

The prompts are as follows:

- My name is _____, and here's what happened...

- My reactions were...

- My life has changed in these ways...

- I am angry at...

- I am most sad about...

- What I regret the most is...

- What I didn't realize was...

- What I remember the most is...

- What I can't get out of my head is...

- If I had a time machine, I would...

- If I were God, I would...

- What has helped me is...

- What hasn't helped me is...

- The hardest part is...

- What I fear now the most is...

- When I think about the future, I think...

- What has changed for me is...

- What I am thankful for now is...

- My next steps for today look like...

Numbing Our Grief

When facing the barbed wire feelings of grief, it's common to want to numb our pain. When working with those grappling with addiction, I find it's often the unprocessed emotional pain of a difficult life event that fuels their addictive behaviors. Alcohol, drugs, sex, food, overspending, and indulgent behaviors of all kinds make some sort of sense in our lives when used as numbing agents. In short, no one would become addicted to these things if they didn't somehow help us out of our pain. Though ineffective for the long haul, these short-term Band-Aids leave many a wandering griever numb but unhealed as they focus on the wrong things. New or resurfacing problem behaviors like addiction will only sideline your progress because to *numb something* is not the same as to *heal it*.

Numbing just delays having to deal with it. And once we're no longer numb, not only do we have the original problems that caused us pain but we also have the consequences of our addictive choices.

By thoroughly healing our pain and injuries, we can reap the benefits. People who are truly healed often remark that they experience an increased sense of integrity, personal growth, more self-respect and self-esteem, greater internal peace, a sense of joy and purpose, and even a new life path. Addiction, on the other hand, paves the way to a land of personal suffering that affects you and those you love. Like Alcoholics Anonymous says, for the person who drinks to stop their pain, "one is too many and a thousand is not enough." If you tend to medicate your heavy feelings rather than get under them to get over them, you may be avoiding dealing with an unhealed trauma or loss. So, rather than asking yourself if you drink too much, I invite you to consider asking yourself these five questions instead. First posed by Sam Dylan Finch in 2017[1], this list provides a good way to tell if your behaviors with drugs, alcohol, spending, sex, and other activities are acting like a numbing gel for life:

1. What are the consequences (of my behavior), and do they matter to me?

2. Am I compromising my values (with my addictive choices)?

---

1 Sam Dylan Finch, "5 Better Questions to Ask Than 'Am I An Alcoholic?'," The Fix, May 19, 2017, https://www.thefix.com/5-better-questions-ask-am-i-alcoholic.

3. What's the outcome of my addictive behaviors? Is it predictable? Am I in control?

4. What are my loved ones telling me (about my choices and behaviors)? Why is that?

5. What is my drinking (drug use, impulsive behaviors, unsafe choices, risky decision-making) trying to tell me?

Once you've taken your own inventory, I invite you to take the answers to these five questions and visit a trusted leader, counselor, or family member for help in deciding what to do next.

Putting Language to Your Loss

At this point, we are trying to get under what is happening on the outside. This will allow you to see your loss and develop a language for your experience of it. Once you complete the Grief Response Checklist, you can see where grief is impacting your life in ways you may not have realized. When these prompts are completed and combined, they create The Story. The simple act of writing these sentences helps you begin to process your loss by understanding what's going on inside your head and your body. You may not even realize there's a story swirling around you. Having some specific footholds will help get you through your loss by understanding what's actually going on and how you're carrying it.

I use both the Grief Response Checklist and The Story with my clients, so they can wrap their heads around what's happening and get clarity about their story. They often come to me not realizing how they react to their loss. They don't know they've been having a grief response. They may exhibit unusual behaviors, feel like they're being punished or losing control, or fear that they'll never feel completely safe again. These are all grief responses.

Often, people experiencing grief don't yet have a language to give voice to their loss. Once you can articulate how your life has changed, you can speak about it to others. Maybe you are angry at the paramedics or the police officer, the gunman or the driver, or you're angry at your loved one for not taking care of themselves and getting sick, or being in that high-risk, abusive relationship. Maybe you don't realize you've been replaying a scene over and over again. You're walking around feeling numb, or you're not romantically involved anymore with your partner. In whatever way grief is impacting you, it's so important to be able to articulate your feelings.

In the next chapter, we will look at ways to take care of yourself as you continue to do your grief work.

Chapter 3

Self-Preservation

"Sometimes you need to move slowly so you can later move powerfully. The modern world is so fast paced that there is pressure to keep up. Setting aside what everyone else is doing and moving at your natural speed will help you make better decisions and lift up your inner peace."

—YUNG PUEBLO

M any a female client in her early- to mid-forties has walked into my office to explain some version of the following story:

I got married, had kids, worked at a job, and played the good wife to my spouse. And now I am tired, angry, and empty. My kids and husband don't appreciate me, I didn't ever get to follow my dreams, no one in the house does as much as I do, and dammit, why after I have done so much, can't someone just do something for me in return? Just once. Don't I matter to anyone?

When people grow up and become parents, for all intents and purposes, they put their own self-development on a shelf while they give birth to and ensure the development of the next generation. Once their kids are old enough to go to school, start a career, or otherwise begin "adulting" for themselves, most parents begin longing for some of their previous life back. With decades of caring for others under their belt, many—women especially—want to reclaim who they were before they became wives or mothers and start growing through their next stages after they've walked the path of self-sacrifice.

The first place we start is getting to the idea that they have a life of their own that needs attending to. Next, we lay out some self-care practices to help gather themselves back up after decades of giving on behalf of their family. Invariably, nearly every client I work with hits a wall when we get to the self-care part. Why?

- They believe self-care is *selfish*.

- They were never shown how to have a good relationship with themselves.

- They have low self-esteem and thought they could gain self-worth and value through their role as a mother, wife, employee, student, career woman, etc.

- They believed it was more important to take care of their family than of themselves.

- There was no time or money or help to give them any space to take care of themselves.

- Work, family, and parenthood are all *very* demanding.

- Self-sacrifice is a noble virtue in our culture and is a mandatory requirement in raising a family or being successful in just about anything.

These women have leveraged themselves for work and family to such a degree that they don't know who they are anymore. The messaging has been so strong, and their valiant dedication to outside forces like kids and jobs is so potent that even when they begin to reclaim themselves, they are flooded with guilt, self-hatred, and negative internal messaging. The important work we do together is similar to what I'll teach in this chapter. Namely, to engage in self-care is to not only find solutions to many of the problems that bring people to therapy (betrayal, job issues, mood instability, divorce, and more), but it also helps those around you. Believe it or not, I often have to give permission, write out assignments, argue with people, and even write prescriptions on a pad of paper to get them to show up for themselves. And when they do, they solve many if not most of their problems and more!

When we place value on ourselves and begin to attend to our struggles, we become our own pattern-interrupters and problem solvers. This is where the magic happens! People remark that they feel well, helped, or empowered by meeting with a therapist and doing the *work* of therapy. Their lives change.

Note: therapy should help move you forward and create change in your life, not just have you talking about how you feel every week.

It all begins with a very intentional practice of self-care called self-preservation. Preserving and caring for oneself is neither selfish nor self-sacrificing; it's something altogether different. Self-preservation can help us begin again, solve problems, grow to our full potential, and take better care of those we love. Anne Lamott, author and TED Talk sensation says, "When we care for ourselves as our very own beloved—with naps, healthy food, clean sheets, a lovely cup of tea—we can begin to give in wildly generous ways to the world, from abundance."

Whatever loss you are recovering from, after you have located yourself on the Grief Response Checklist and written out your Story, the next step I recommend is a set of personalized self-care skills you can use to anchor and preserve yourself as you travel this difficult path. Why? The process of loss may bring up a lot of vulnerability or sadness—as it would for anybody who gets to the core of their grief experience—so it's important to go back to home base and tune in to yourself to develop a new practice of self-care in times of difficulty. But that's not what people in dark grieving typically do. Free-falling in their heartache, they tend rather to gravitate toward a state of self-neglect when it comes to tenderness toward themselves.

When we're sad, we tend to forego the care we would normally give ourselves. Sometimes those who are deep in the underbelly of distress may forget to eat, will oversleep or sleep too little, will fail to bathe, and sometimes can't even brush their teeth or leave the house. It's normal and common for someone experiencing loss to let the big and little parts of their life go because the grief is so shocking and overwhelming. As a result, their inner light dims, they feel a sense of wreckage around them, and they abandon themselves. While this is a typical response, I invite you consider a few suggestions that might make sense for you at this time.

The rationale for engaging in self-care, even though we're devastated, is mostly related to others. I say this because many of us (especially women) refrain from doing things for ourselves in general, but especially during hard times. We are raised by society to please others while at the same time, our hormones drive us to nurture others. The result: we care deeply for other people, often to our own detriment. The result: self-neglect. Just ask any parent or family member of someone battling an addiction. The time-tested mandate for all co-addicts is learning how to *detach with love*. In doing so, a ripple effect is created around the one who struggles, and the sick loved one may (finally) see reality and take stock of their lives. Pleasing and nurturing others is a beautiful expression of the human spirit but not when it handicaps those around us and especially not when it's at the expense of our own self.

Engaging in acts of self-preservation through the practice of what Lamott refers to as *radical self-care* is a gift to those around you. When you value and prioritize yourself, you fill your own cup, and in doing so, take others off the hook from having to do it for you. You also release them from the resentments and blame we all accidentally carry toward others who we perceive *should* be taking care of us the way we've taken care of them. By stepping into a *preserve myself* mindset, you become good medicine for yourself and others. When you model to your loved ones that you have value and are worth preserving, a ripple effect occurs. When they see that you relate to yourself as you would a good friend, their view of you can't help but widen. Your love and tender care toward your body, mind, and spirit sets a tone for *their* care of you as well. Ultimately, your survival maneuvers of self-preservation also impact the way they view themselves. Children of parents who prioritize self-respect as a driving value are more likely to do the same than kids whose parents engage in self-hatred and neglect.

If self-care isn't automatic for you, then do it for those you love. We are all deeply entangled with those closest to us via friendships, children, families, and romantic partnerships. Your loved ones are watching you and will organize themselves the same way you do. In cases like this, I often look to nature as a guide.

Starlings are tiny birds who travel in huge flocks. To protect themselves from predators, starlings not only congregate by the thousands but fly in a synchronized pattern called a murmuration. The murmuration effect, like billowing smoke, creates an eerie phenomenon in the sky. Like a huge dark sheet blowing in the wind on a backyard clothes hanger, the murmuration confuses predators and ensures survival. When predators target an attack on one bird, every other bird around it becomes a collective wonder on its behalf. Sensing a threat, the birds nearest the predator respond with an array of tactical maneuvers—the slight tilt of a wing, the turn of a head, or a slowing of speed—tapping out a survival message to the other birds to avoid the menace. The next layer of birds does the same. Each tiny creature is adept at watching the seven closest birds to itself and shadowing their movement.

Moving ten times faster than any airplane, these formation flyers achieve such synchronicity to the others that they confuse and outwit their predators. In one another's presence, through sharp attunement, they mimic the patterns of the other and echo those changes to everyone around them. Their entanglements with one another are not just messages on how to behave, but a split-second, spirited bulletin that can mean the difference between life and death. In essence, if you attend to your own needs, you'll create a murmuration effect and foil the local "falcons" of your life.

Perhaps you've been thrown into your loss and are not accustomed to taking care of yourself. Maybe, like many of my clients, you've been going through life prioritizing kids, family, career, partner, job, degree, all these things that pull energy from you, but no energy is reciprocated or refilled. Or maybe no one ever taught you how to prioritize yourself, or you had a mother who was so self-sacrificing that you thought martyrdom was the only way to live. Maybe you feel guilty when you take time for yourself, or you have self-hatred or are dismissive of your needs, just like the family you came from was dismissive of you. All these old patterns and behaviors have caused you to self-avoid, and now you are here in the wake of your grief. Perfect. I'm so glad you're here with me. This terrible event, the thing you lost and are grieving, may help you finally draw a line in the sand where for the first time, you begin to show up for yourself...even just a little bit.

The first gift of this grief may be that you learn to acknowledge, feel, and sit with your own needs, and then you learn what it's like to see yourself in need and meet those needs to care for yourself as you would for those you love. It's quite possible that your devastation may be the dawn of a relationship with yourself you never thought possible. This could be an unintended positive of your loss. Like a tiny starling, when the enemies of your soul lock onto you and your clan, your new practice of self-preservation can render your tribe safe.

Kobe Bryant's wife Vanessa could see it. She shared about the three children who need all the love and support she has to give right now. She has control over being grateful and focusing on the lives of her husband Kobe and her daughter Gianna rather than on their deaths. In the middle of grief, it's important to identify that we probably feel a lack of control, especially if the loss was sudden, abrupt, and unexpected. To regain our balance and to steady ourselves, it's important to identify where we do have control. You have control over how you take care of yourself and what you do next. Now, let's look at how you can make that happen.

CREATING MARGIN

I have developed my own self-care rituals. Brené Brown uses what she calls *permission slips* to gain the energy she needs to prioritize herself; I call it *having margin.* One way to set the stage for taking back some control over your life is to create margin for yourself. Richard Swenson, who wrote the book *Margin,* says margin is to "restore emotional, physical, financial, and time reserves to our overloaded lives." Like the page you are reading, along the perimeter of the written text, there is an obligatory emptiness where no words should be. Usually just a few inches wide, the white space around the edges of a page denotes where words end, and clean space begins. This clean space was meant to give the reader's eye a rest before moving down to the next line of words. Occasionally, a reader will also use it to scribble a note or will bend the top edge down to hold their place in the story. It's almost always used to house the page numbers, insert footnotes, and to bind and flip the pages once they're made into a book. What if you were reading this book and there were words running amok across every page, squeezing out any room for the page numbers, chapter titles, or a place to write a note or two? Most readers would become frustrated or overwhelmed and never read another word. The book's message, even if it was a great one, would be totally lost by its lack of boundaries.

There are a variety of uses for this seemingly idle thing called a margin. Our phones and emails even use margin. Can you imagine being in a group text where everyone's replies ran together with no way to separate them? Confusion and frustration would be the result. To have clean space between one thing ending and another beginning is the preferred, even expected, standard in our world. Margins are so common we never even notice them anymore, like the lines on a freeway denoting car lanes. We have unspoken expectations that they should be there and feel frantic when they aren't.

"Margin," says Swenson, "is the space that exists between ourselves and our limits." But so many of us lack the ability to give ourselves breathing room and to develop some blank parts of our own page. During a challenging life event, we are more likely than ever to neglect the white space of our existence. When substantial harm and loss occur, the white space on the paper of who we are shrinks considerably.

I build my life around having enough margin to practice my self-care habits. Sometimes my "permission slip" or *margin* looks like taking a warm bath, wrapping up in a soft blanket on the couch, wearing a certain pair of pajamas, and going to bed early. Other times, it's pressing through and finishing a project so I have the mental rest that comes from knowing I've cleared my plate of my to-do list. Still other times, I take responsibility for my needs by letting those around me know what is happening. When I feel the effects of grief, I am honest with my family, but make sure not to overwhelm them. For instance, if anybody asks me how I'm doing, part of having margin means answering them honestly and specifically. If I had a hard night, I might say something like, "I did not sleep well last night, so I may take a nap today." If the feelings of loss are particularly strong or I am remembering the event and processing through some of that grief, I might say, "I'm feeling kind of low; I have some things I need to do to take care of myself. I'll do those and I'll be OK, but just so you know, I'm not feeling like myself." And everybody who knows me knows that there's nothing they need to do for me. I don't put anybody else on the hook to feel bad or take care of me; I am not expecting them to fix it. *I* take responsibility for the situation.

In Chapter 1, I wrote about how we deal with grief as a society: we are so focused on productivity that there isn't a lot of room to have a bad day. I could push through like nobody's business, but I think pushing made me sick. Avoiding grief, pushing through for the purpose of "getting stuff done," and trying to be all things for all people led me to catastrophic illness. I didn't see what was happening because I continually put myself on the back burner. There is a price to be paid. Everyone pays a different price; mine was illness. Others pay with drug addiction or infidelity or by being horrible to live with.

Your grief is going to come out in one way or the other.

Rather than neglecting and sidelining yourself through it, what if instead, you and I made a plan to care for yourself through this storyline of loss? If you can develop just a bit of white space around your story, things will be a little easier for you and you'll be easier to live with, too. But first, it's important that we talk about your foe in this process: *guilt*.

RELINQUISHING GUILT

When embarking on the journey away from self-neglect, most people I know are besieged by pangs of guilt that push them away from themselves and back into a self-avoiding mindset.

Don't get me wrong; putting others first, serving those we love, doing a good job, finishing what we start, and securing the well-being of our family and friends is crucial to the survival of our households and communities. I'm not talking about the guilt you feel when you do a bad job, break the rules, violate your values, or hurt someone you love. Guilt, when it's signaling that we are out of integrity, can act like an indicator light on our dashboard; something's not right. The guilt I'm referring to is the sensation you feel when you have taken care of your responsibilities—for your children, your employer, your clients, your parents, or your spouse—and now you are taking some time for yourself. I'm talking about the guilt you feel for saying no to one more commitment. This is that blame you feel when you take a little for yourself rather than always giving to someone else. Most women are "pack animals" and if there is someone in need—especially a dear friend, neighbor, or family member—a woman will instinctively prioritize another's needs over her own. We need outside signs that it is OK, and in fact quite crucial, to be a good neighbor to ourselves. So, because we are more awash with guilt than with awareness of our own needs, I recommend we let guilt be our guide.

When you set out to practice any of the recommended skills below, and you are met with a barrage of guilty thoughts that encourage you to leave the practice, good news! You are onto something. One of the best ways for us to know our boundaries are working and that our self-neglect is under attack is when we feel guilty.

I'm not trying to get you to neglect your responsibilities; what I'm suggesting is that you take on *more* responsibility for yourself, your needs, and your care rather than burning yourself out and blaming everyone around you for not seeing you struggle. This is *your* life. It's time to realign it, and you can do this by noticing how you move away from yourself and back into self-sacrifice mode because of the presence of guilt. Once the guilt hits, let that sensation tell you to stay with the practices below—you're on the right track!

YOUR MARGIN TOOL KIT

Here is a list of structured self-care tools to help you add margin when you're ready.

PLEASE Skills

PLEASE is an acronym for more than a half dozen self-care to-dos in an easy-to-remember format (e.g., *Do your PLEASE skills*). The PLEASE skills come from Dialectical Behavioral

Therapy. This therapy, referred to as DBT, aims to teach people how to live in the moment, develop healthy ways to cope with stress, regulate emotions, and improve their relationships with self and others. The goal of the PLEASE skills is to get you busy taking care of you. The six letters and their corresponding directives are meant to be practiced together as a whole. Some people have a hard time taking on all six letters, so start where you are and work from there. For some of us, the PLEASE skills are a breeze. Great! Keep reading for ways to deepen your practice of befriending yourself.

P is to take care of the physical body—shower, brush your teeth and hair, wash your face, put on clean clothes.

L is to treat any *illnesses* you might have. If you need to go to the doctor because you have strep throat or a pain in your side, go. If you need therapy, go. Use your medication as prescribed. Go see a dentist.

E is to *eat regularly*. Try to get three balanced meals a day, plus snacks. Avoid sugar and salt, and eat meals that are healthy and nourishing.

A is to *avoid* mood-altering substances. Also *avoid avoiding*. Avoiding is a survival pattern. You may be avoiding difficult conversations. You may be avoiding taking care of yourself. You may avoid paying the bills. Avoid what's not working for you, and avoid avoiding what *does* work for you.

S is *sleep*. Rest when needed, even if that means taking a nap during the day. Get a proper amount of sleep for your body. If you are unable to sleep, there is a lot of research around the benefits of getting into a dark, quiet room and lying down, closing your eyes, and breathing deeply. Even if you're not in a deep sleep, your brain is still able to reset and regenerate to help you feel rested.

E is *exercise* or stretch. Move your body in ways that feel good. A goal to reach for is at least twenty minutes a day of exercising or stretching as a starting point.

If you're doing the PLEASE skills and still can't seem to get through your day, or the depression is overwhelming, you can't stop crying, you can't get out of bed, or other areas of your life, such as finances or relationships, are disrupted, it's time to escalate the matter. But first, breathe. Just take a few deep breaths. Being paralyzed by heavy emotions during times of loss is normal. You might not be ready to move yet. That's OK. When you are, here are some next steps:

- Take yourself to see a therapist, clergy, or a safe leader.

- Attend a support group related to the loss you have experienced.

- If your budget allows, get a massage or a facial.

- Take a brief break from your tasks (fifteen minutes to two hours).

- Take some time off work, and/or ask someone to help with the kids.

- Let a trusted person know how you're doing at that very moment when grief feels heavy or like you can't move out of it.

My Margin

I've developed a list of practices that have been effective for me over the years. There are nine items on my self-care list. When life has thrown me on the ropes, I get back on my feet with these specific practices. If you'd like to borrow some from me as you build margin around your story, give these a try:

- Spend time in friendships which are mutually fulfilling.

- Go to bed early or try sleeping in.

- Take a long, hot bath.

- Walk on the beach and forest bathe on a hike or walk.

- Set limits with your work schedule.

- Practice tenderheartedness for yourself by placing your hand over your heart when you feel afraid.

- Ask for and receive physical love (hugs, hands, holds).

- Be intentional about spirituality.

- Seek laughter as often as possible.

Simplified Self-Care

You may think taking care of yourself is expensive, but it doesn't have to be. Having a bath, taking a nap, calling a friend, going for a walk, reading, writing in a journal: none of these cost any money. Likewise, it doesn't have to be time-consuming. I know a lot of people that feel great in simply making their bed, showering, and getting ready for the day, even if they are working at home. That ritual feels important for them to be or feel their best.

Instant Mood Shifter

If you are *not* in a particularly dark corridor of your loss but more of a "meh" phase and want to feel a bit better, some instant mood shifters may be exactly what you need. This list will be especially helpful for you now that you've gotten under all the symptoms of your loss response in the previous chapter:

- Look at favorite photos.

- Watch silly videos.

- Read inspirational quotes and poems.

- Listen to comforting music (I have a feel-good playlist).

- Create or view inspiring art.

- Write about your experience.

- Connect with animals or nature.

- Watch a beautiful sunset.

- Take a walk in the woods.

- Spend time playing with a pet.

- Work in the garden.

ALLOW SKILLS

Allow myself to tell people how much I love, admire, and care for them. There is a lot of science around telling a loved one how we feel about them. We may feel grateful for or admire someone, but often we don't communicate it in a way that's meaningful to the one we admire. One of the best ways to care for ourselves, fill our own cup, and get outside of our heads is by connecting with people we love and telling them what we love about them. Send a thank-you note or a kind text, give a hug, and let someone know how much you appreciate them today.

Allow myself to give and receive random acts of kindness. Decide for yourself what this might look like. For example, if you're in a drive-through, you can pay the cashier for the next person's order. Same thing at a grocery store. If you see a delivery driver, paramedic, doctor, police officer, nurse, or fireman in public about to go eat, you could pay for their meal, buy them a coffee, or just walk up to them and thank them.

Allow yourself to find your faith or religion comforting to you. I say *allow* here because sometimes we get stuck in our faith during times of loss. The reasons that brought you to this book may have pulled the rug right out from under your understanding of spiritual things. You may be feeling dismally adrift in your faith rather than strong and trusting. If your cataclysms have brought up questions about eternity or about whether God exists, here's something to try:

A way to interact with your spiritual pondering might be a Wise Mind practice from DBT. The Wise Mind is defined as the meeting of the emotional mind and reasonable mind. It's the ability to see the value in both reason and emotion and choose the middle ground. When we access our inner wisdom, we say we are in Wise Mind. Tonight, as you are going to bed, try offering up one of your questions to Wise Mind. Your Wise Mind, the part of you that naturally seeks something higher, may awaken you with an answer.

In the morning, pause for a moment and revisit the question you asked the night before. As you relisten to your own questions, see if a response is made available in your thoughts. Are you hearing the echo of an answer within? A phrase or words that seem to make sense? Perhaps it's a desire to go hiking in the mountains, sit in the serene quiet, and notice the beauty and the vastness around you. Do you notice if there's a longing for your faith traditions? If words begin bubbling to the surface within you, it might feel a lot like prayer.

Keep going with these questions and the Wise Mind process. These are all seeds growing in you that I want to encourage you to continue watering. I love what author Michael Singer says, that "God is an experience" and not a study, an essay, a building, or an argument. Your Wise Mind may be directing you to places and actions that will help you experience God.

Other Things I Have Allowed Space For:

- Practicing the rituals of my faith

- Sitting down to pray, even if I don't have a lot of words

- Gathering (online or in person) with a community of people who share my faith

- Listening to hymns and songs that inspire me

- Being in a sacred space

- Seeing the emblems of my faith

We can still be angry at life and want to leave and run away from and punish whoever is in charge for what has happened and—at the exact same time—find comfort in our faith. The two can coexist. Allow space for all of it.

A SPECIFIC TIME TO CRY

Allocating time to cry helps me function. I can carry my burdens throughout the day if I know I have a cry-time coming soon. By giving myself a space and time to grieve, I have affirmed my need to process and release my heavy emotions. For example, telling myself that *from 5:00 p.m. to 6:00 p.m., I'm going into my bedroom to wail and lament and have a heavy, ugly, face-down cry* feels so reassuring. When I put a timebox around my feelings and needs, I feel less overwhelmed by them. Timeboxes allow us to respond as if we have permission to feel all we need to feel for a period of time, but not forever.

I feel so contained and secure when I give myself a timeframe to *feel* my anguish. I know now that my losses need to be let out, or they'll pile up inside of me and cause me harm. Like an outdoor faucet with a spray hose, it's as if my emotions have been turned on but the nozzle is closed. The pressure and intensity build up and must go somewhere. I can't function or think straight if I don't release the pressure.

Exercise

Set aside a specific time to cry, and designate a "Sad Space" in your home. We use time slots on calendars for everything from getting our hair done, meetings with our boss, seeing friends, and even taking our pet to the groomers. Why not schedule a time to cry as well?

CRY CLOSET

Emotions are indicator lights on the dashboard of our lives.

Years ago, I knew that a heavy cry helped me. Every time I'd try to fight it and push through it, it would backfire; I'd end up overwhelmed or in physical pain, or I'd have wild mood swings. But when I engaged with my emotions and gave them space to breathe and be felt, though gutting in the moment, the eventual result was a sense of relief.

My bedroom closet has become a bit of a birthing room for my heavier feelings that are ready to come out. Though all my children have seen me cry, and I make no apologies for heavy tears or other intense emotions, I also try not to engulf my family with the intensity of my feelings. My feelings and what I do with them are my responsibility. I have several options to manage them, many of which you are seeing in this book, and I can invoke any number of strategies to work through them and understand why they are there, but ultimately, it's up to me to manage them.

One of the ways I do this is by helping my overwhelming sadness to move through me. I set aside a special time and place to listen deeply to why that sadness is there. By bringing it forth from within, and bearing witness to its messages, I give it safe passage as it leaves. The crying is sometimes about a specific person or event. Other times, it's about stress relief. But always, it feels to me like a process of being cleansed. If Marie Kondo, an organization expert, were by my side, she and I together might say, "Thank you, sadness, shame and loss. You have been of good service to me in helping me lose, reflect, grow, and change. Now, I am cleaning you out. You must go, so I can make room for newer things that spark joy."

In our home, it is well known and accepted that a "good cry" can clear the clutter of the soul. I have let all my kids know that I'm just taking care of myself and feeling my feelings and that I am OK. I also let my husband know exactly what I need through the beginning, middle, and end of my cry.

Setting up a time to cry, designating a special place for it, and letting those I care about know what I need is definitely a way to take care of myself. I most often observe that the pressure of my losses and struggles are backing up in me when my body talks to me. The presence of gripping shoulder pain, a migraine, a notable lack of energy, or thoughts that spiral dark and downward are all signals that I must attend to my internal pressures and release the burdens inside of me.

Knowing I won't be walking around feeling heavy and sad all the time because I've taken the time to put bookends around this sacred space, grieving feels manageable to me and my family. In the past, hearing me cry in my room would set my children on an edge of worry and concern. It was unsettling for them. They didn't know if I was OK. My husband used to think there was something wrong with me, that he had hurt me, or that I was suffering and needed help. Sometimes that was true. If we've been in relationships for any amount of time, our partners and loved ones do wind up hurting us, and the natural response to that is to feel sad and cry. But what a gift to give those you love: a guidebook to your grief. Specifically, here's what I need, what I don't need, and when this will happen.

I know it's not always possible to schedule such things, and of course, depending on the timing of your loss, there may be no way to contain the edges of your pain. But wouldn't an intentional practice of listening to yourself, attending to what you need, and letting a few others in on it be so good for you?

CAUTION TAPE

Still, there are other times—sometimes days and weeks at a time—when the hurt, sorrow, and even anger will not let up. This is to be expected in times of grief and loss. A practice in our home is to declare a zone around oneself and tell the others, "You may want to put some caution tape around me. I do not feel well. I may be grumpy, cry, or even lash out. I'm sorry in advance; I'm doing my best." Basically, we all know we're not fit to be around other people at that moment and don't want to hurt anyone else while we are sidelined. Each time we have the "caution tape" conversation, everyone in our home knows to give the person some space and to not take anything they say, do, or don't do too personally. We also allow for about three days of "flu-like" behavior when one of us is struggling through something. We let the one who is grappling with a difficulty off-the-hook, so to speak, from any expectations we might have of them. Instead, we bring them blankets or their favorite meal, we use softer, gentler words, and when they're ready, we hug them. This is also where the famous Finch Family Pets go to work.

PET-SOOTHE

In our family, almost any day of the week, you'll find a cat or dog curled up in a lap, lying on a bed, wrapped up in a blanket next to us, or walking alongside us around the house. Connecting with my pets is one of my all-time favorite ways to self-soothe and work on my soul-building. I define *soul-building* as the process of going through and surviving soul-crushing events that tear you down, gut you out, crack you open, and burn you up. But here's the catch: through the teardown process, our tragedies are meant not just to tear us down but to create something in us, too. Author and business leader Ray Dalio says, "Pain + Reflection = Progress." The furry footed Finch Family Pets are truly the facilitators of this process in our family. If pain leads to progress, at our house, there will be a pet helping that process along. Our pets create raucous laughter with their antics, hours of free entertainment with their play, comfort when we're sad, companionship when loneliness hits, and a medium for talking about hard things.

Our pets are like family to us. When nine-pound Chihuahua "Bella" came into our lives from a local shelter, none of us knew she would companion us through the wreckage of 2020. Not only did the pandemic, the riots, and the upheaval of the political climate fall heavily on all of us that year but Darin's brother would also lose his life to suicide, and his dad would die from cancer just a few months later. Bella's intuitive sensitivity and penchant for cuddling was just the solace we all needed as life fell hard on our home.

PUPPY MIND

One time, after a particularly intense period of pain and grief, I just couldn't think straight. I felt detached from reality. We had just come from a memorial for my son's best friend Colin, who was like a son to me and had died suddenly on his motorcycle, only five minutes after leaving our home. Back at work, three of my clients had also died in one week. I was so numb. I was consistently doing the nine items on my self-care list, and I still felt gutted. My husband said, "I'm worried about you. You're not your normal self." One thing you can do is accept that the way you are feeling may just be a part of the grief, but in this case, I needed to do more. I decided to take a leave of absence from work.

Once on leave, I began spending some days just walking on the beach with my dog. Though it was February, the cool weather didn't deter me. Even in the cold, the California seashore is famous for soothing minds and healing souls. I was drawn to it and hoped it would help. I needed something fresh and open to help me think straight.

I stepped out of the car and toward the wintry beach with Bella. Her excited tugs at the leash gave me a reason to walk as we moved from the car and down the cement steps that led from the iconic Pacific Coast Highway to the water.

Bella and I headed toward Huntington Dog Beach, a generous portion of untouched coast where dogs and their fond families can play, run, sun, and walk together off-leash in the waves or on the sand, any day of the week. As I stopped to get a doggy bag, I surveyed this stark, usually-busy-but-now-deserted Southern California playground. As we made our way past the soft upper sand and down to the low-tide-water line, our steps picked up. Hers came in wild leaps and darting runs as she exploded into the freedom of this place, leash and collar off, her small brown legs filled with glee, sniffing at all things new in the sand. With my pant legs pulled up, I walked to the shoreline. A light arose in me as I leaned into Bella's joy, hoping some of her revelry would echo back at me and relieve my stress.

I was three days into my leave of absence and looking for relief from the sore state of my soul. But even on the beach, I felt jumpy and frantic, like I had drunk four cups of black coffee on an empty stomach. But I hadn't. What sparked my nerves was the bad news about my clients, the gutting pain of losing Colin, and my worry that more bad things would happen. My mind whizzed as I wondered when the other shoe would drop. Initially, just being at the beach helped calm my nerves. But after several minutes, my thoughts started to stir again, and I could feel my heart begin to thump louder when the worry thoughts kicked back in. My body and mind were in sync. Fear-based thoughts created tension, and in response, my heart jumped into high gear and beat wildly. The faster my heart raced, the more fearful my thoughts became. Nothing in my surroundings had changed, only the dance inside my head. And none of it was based on fact; it was just a feedback loop between my thoughts and my body. It was then that I remembered a concept I teach my clients: mindfulness.

A LESSON IN MINDFULNESS

To bring some relief to my thoughts, I called up the practice of mindfulness, a modern mental panacea based on ancient traditions of stilling the mind. According to the practice, we can heal and restore our minds by bringing them consistently back into the present moment. The discipline requires that we attend to just the moment we are in, and nothing else. Regrets from the past and worries about the future fall away when we draw ourselves into the "now."

When undisciplined, our minds are like young dogs: bouncy, fast, and prone to chew on things they shouldn't. I like to call this Puppy Mind. When we are in our Puppy Mind, we tend to chew on past hurts, worry about things that haven't happened yet, and generally find ourselves at the mercy of our thoughts, which are often based on fear and catastrophic projections rather than fact.

Author Michael Singer says, "There is nothing more important to true growth than realizing that you are not the voice of the mind— you are the one who hears it."

Eckhart Tolle echoes this when he writes, "What a liberation to know that the voice in my head is not who I am." You see, there are really two selves in our minds, the one who notices what's happening and the one it's happening to. I'm not going into a deep philosophical discussion about these things. Volumes have been written about this by folks who study this as their full-time work. My point is that once we realize our thoughts are not really *us* and are not permanent and are instead things we can change, work with, amend, improve, stop, and control...life gets better. Way better. This is the benefit of practicing mindfulness— we can see that what's happening inside us is not as we wish it to be and that we are hurting because of it. A wild Puppy Mind can be made to behave, and everyone is happier.

The best thing to do with a Puppy Mind is put it on a leash. For instance, with a new puppy, most owners establish limits about where the puppy sleeps, eats, plays, and poops.

New puppies may also go to puppy classes to learn to obey their owners, stay safe, and be a good friend to their family and other dogs. By doing this, the puppy knows what to do and how to do it to stay safe and have fun. Likewise, these are important things to do with our thoughts. While we buy leashes, crates, fences, and chew toys for our pets, we often don't set boundaries for our own minds. Current research on the prevalence of anxiety and depression in our culture is evidence of this. Mindfulness is one way to help tame your Puppy Mind.

By telling our minds what to think moment by moment, we can control the flow of thoughts, cut down the negative ones, and even alter our mood. But like in dog obedience school, it takes practice. With the help of mindfulness, I put my mind on the leash of the present moment that day at the beach. Taking a deep breath, I steadied myself to exactly what was happening that moment and how it felt in my body.

Second by second, as I stood up and began to walk along the shore, I thought to myself *OK, ground yourself. That's the first step. Just notice where you are, and feel your feet on the wet, firm sand as you walk. Feel the chilled winter air on your face, hear the roll of the waves, and watch the dogs have fun. Be here now. The rest will come later.* I knew that as the father of mindfulness Jon Kabat-Zinn explains, the only way I could befriend myself and this experience was to become mindful of what was happening.

Once the mindfulness of the moment clicked in, I found myself following all sorts of things on purpose, one at a time, in the present moment. Suddenly, my practice involved the swooping seagulls flying across the sky. They held my attention for a few minutes. Then, three small dogs giving chase in a wide and barking circle around their owner caught my eye. I marveled at how two of them leaped into the waves to catch each other, but how one would dodge the water altogether. In the distance, I focused on the dark outline of a group of surfers poised on the flat water, waiting for waves to roll in. I let my attention rest there, remembering that my mind could only hold one thought at a time. In doing so, the panic and worry and the catastrophes that had been in my body, in my flesh, and in my mind had to stay at bay. I watched the surfers; I studied their position. I saw them bounce on the water at least for a full five minutes. I took it all in, second by second, the sound, the smell, and the feel of the dog beach. And while five minutes wasn't that long, it was long enough to help heal my mind that day. The panic thoughts were gone.

When I pulled my attention back to my body, my earlier thought patterns, which had felt like wildfire, had disappeared. My breathing had naturally slowed down; I could feel my heartbeat soften, and a sense of well-being take over. Taking in my beach experience moment by moment had become like a metronome for my soul. My whole system had taken on a peaceful rhythm, and finally, I felt safe.

So, most any time a person in our home is turned inside out about something, our practices of intentional crying (mostly me), space-giving, caution tape, three flu-like days, and pet therapy are all used as needed. I have even been known to give my kids a mental health day off from school and take the same time for myself if needed. Pushing through, avoiding the pain, and acting "fine" when something is clearly wrong does happen, has to happen, sometimes. But an invitation to step into more margin and let the pain breathe, so to speak, and practice mindfulness is now a part of our family's values.

COPING THROUGH DARK GRIEVING

An extension of the Puppy Mind problem is when our grief runs dark. There is a time to just grieve of course, to feel sad, feel the loss, cry, be forlorn, go to bed, suffer in our devastation, and delegate responsibilities to others. But if that time leads to feeling overwhelmed by negative memories of the past, and what we call *time-sliding* or ruminations, a good practice is to learn to ground and reorient ourselves in the present moment. Time-sliding is when the mind replays old memories that make us feel worse, and ruminations are when the brain is constantly reenacting one of the difficulties of the loss (like the intersection where they died, the courtroom where your divorce was finalized, the moment that your boss told you about your job loss, the scene of the crime, or when that person broke up with you). Time-sliding and ruminations about our losses are normal. But sometimes they can turn dangerous if we are flooded with regret and despair over what happened, and it won't let up. This is where good, normal grief can turn bad. Some of us are more prone to heavy emotions than others. Sadness may turn easily to hopelessness and/or death. This is a darker type of grieving.

Dark Grief is waiting in the wings for some of us more than others. I've known people who have been so overcome by loss that they start contemplating suicide or even acting on those urges. This is why it's important to have an exit route when depression, discouragement, and despair show up and hang out for too long. I refer to these three cohorts as the Three Ds. We can expect to be under their grip from time to time, but when theirs are the only voices we can hear, we must try and reach for another way of thinking.

Grounding Exercises

"Grounding" is a technique used in yoga practices, meditation and breathwork, contemplative prayer, and in therapy. When a person is flooded with overwhelming thoughts or emotions, it's essential to help them ground to something stable and real—like the floor, the chair, and their body. This way, the surge of thoughts and emotions can be directed to focus on one thing at a time, like I did at the dog beach with Bella. Within a few minutes of focused thought and anchoring, the brain and nervous system can settle down and realign themselves.

To ground yourself, try this five-part technique:

1. Refocus your attention solely on the environment around you. Where are you? Who are you with? What sounds do you hear? What's the temperature? What's the view, etc.?

2. Find one color in the room (blue, let's say), and focus your thoughts only on naming everything you find in the room that is also blue. Then move on to red, orange, yellow, and so forth. When your mind jumps out of this grounding exercise (because it will, it's a wild puppy), gently redirect it to the assignment at hand. You may need to redirect it twenty times; that's OK. You're building a new muscle—the puppy is learning to behave!

3. With intention, feel all ten of your toes on the ground. Then, do a body scan that brings your attention to your feet, up your legs, and on to each body part up to the

top of your head. Again, keep the leash on your mind, and stay on the path with this. Your mind is learning.

4. Practice paced breathing. Paced breathing is slow, deep, diaphragmatic breathing. With normal breathing, you take about twelve to fourteen breaths a minute. By comparison, paced breathing requires only five to seven breaths a minute. The paced breaths are slow, smooth, and deep enough to move your diaphragm. The goal of paced breathing is to reduce the stress chemicals your brain produces and facilitate a relaxation response.

5. Change your self-talk by telling yourself in the moment, "I am safe right now, and this will pass," and repeating it if necessary.

Additional Coping Strategies

1. Download and use a calming or mindfulness app on your phone.

2. If you find yourself barraged by negative memories, ruminating, lost in corrosive thoughts, or time-sliding, or you can't get yourself moving at all, get up and get going. Let's say you're alone in your room, or you've isolated at home. Get on the phone. Walk out of your room. Taking physical steps is important, so you can rivet your attention on a sensory experience. Either hearing someone else's voice, seeing someone else's

face, or physically moving your body will help to unhook the wicked rhythm in your head that might be beyond regular grieving.

3. Next, imagine in your mind moving toward a future outlook of a stronger sense of yourself. This one may feel a little vague, but it is nothing more than—in that moment—closing your eyes and picturing positive actions you can take. Picture yourself getting up, taking a shower, and sleeping well tonight. Imagine yourself stepping out of your bedroom, walking out on your front porch, getting into your garden, or going to Target. Picture where you want to be so that your brain can feel the energy and pull in that direction. If the dark abyss of grief feels dangerous for you, this might make it easier for you to get active in the moment.

HOT SPOTS

Identifying what I call a *hot spot* is another tool to help you deal with your grief. In the running world, a hot spot is a blister-in-waiting, and it's usually a sign the blister will be painful and deep. Under the siege of rub, pressure, and time by the runner's shoe, especially during long runs, the skin begins to swell and become painful. Without a proper covering, the hot spot will erupt into a small, painful lesion on the skin, filled with fluid and angst for the athlete. This section is about identifying the traumas that happened during our loss that have led to complex anguish and a sense of being *stuck* in it.

After I wrote the previous section, I walked downstairs in my home to stretch my legs and gather my thoughts on the next section. As I came down to the middle landing between two sets of stairs, I saw the latest copy of *People* magazine on our coffee table. The bright, young face of Chadwick Boseman stared back at me. In the lead role of T'Challa, Boseman brought us all things Wakanda in *The Black Panther*, the hit film that earned Marvel its first Oscar. Days earlier, I had read the sad story of his death from colon cancer, and with a little clicking, I came across an Instagram video he'd recorded that eventually had to be removed because of the online hatred and judgment posted in the comments.

In April 2020, after he had posted a video promoting donations to Operation 42, a charity to help fight COVID-19, some fans expressed concerns about his considerable weight loss and wished him well. But others, including cruel, reckless folks known as internet trolls and several media outlets, began a bully campaign by labeling him the *Crack Panther*.

Swirling rumors about Boseman's weight loss and possible drug use forced the celebrity to remove the post. He had kept his battle with cancer private, sharing only with his closest friends and family members. But in the last few months of his life, while he was hopefully making some peace with the outcome of his four-year battle with cancer, others on the outside of his storyline said and thought the worst.

Certainly, those careless and cruel remarks made the grief process worse for him and everyone close to him. And in the midst of that, do you think Chadwick Boseman's family cared about the model of grief? They were likely feeling all of the Big Five, but mostly they'd be heartbroken, walking around numb and in pain.

Their sweet Chad posted an open-hearted invitation to do good in the world, only to be met with piss and rant. Though time may indeed heal much of their pain (and I hope it does), the injustice of a loved one being bullied while also dying may be with them for years to come. It will become a *hot spot* of their story.

Often warm and tender to the touch, hot spots make every runner's experience more painful. The extra difficult or cruel things that happen to us in the storyline of our grief are like hot spots on the heels of a marathon runner. When we're faced with multiple cruel happenings during a loss, like the betrayal of a friend or partner; a hurtful healthcare worker; an absent, negligent, or abusive family member; a perpetrator set free; or online bullies during our final weeks of life, sometimes these hot spots are all we can focus on. Hot spots make working through grief that much harder. And once we begin to unpack our storyline of grief, it's often these hot spots we remember the most. Bessel van der Kolk, a leader in trauma treatment said, "Neuroscience research shows that the only way we can change the way we feel is by becoming aware of our inner experience and learning to befriend what is going inside ourselves." When we identify and take action around the hot spots of our own story, we can indeed become aware of and start to befriend these parts of ourselves, and in doing so, we lessen their hold on us.

I had a grueling hospitalization once that took me away from my family for days on end. The many medical procedures I had and the "from-bad-to-worse" state of my heart and lung conditions seemed overwhelming at the time. But three things stand out as the worst parts (the hot spots) to me from those days:

1. A mistake a resident physician made that sent me into respiratory arrest and nearly cost me my life.

2. A hospital roommate who attempted suicide the second night we were housed together.

3. A transport orderly who left me in the hallway in a wheelchair at night outside the CT scan room, alone for two hours. Right before he left, he also told me that the morgue was just down the hall.

Professionals in my field would refer to these events as *traumatic experiences*. And they were. But they were also things that made the primary trauma of being a young heart/lung patient away from my loved ones in a hospital even harder. My clients have told me of other hot spot experiences for them. For example, a mother we'll call Lauren called me the night her twenty-four-year-old daughter died. She called from her daughter's apartment, where she distinctly remembers the police *not* allowing her to see her daughter's dead body. She was kept from her while paramedics put her in a body bag and wheeled her out onto the sidewalk and into their ambulance.

Not being able to see her one last time and touch the face of the child she had given birth to seemed unimaginable to her. Of all the many things that happened on that dreadful night, that particular grievance stayed with her more than any of the others. She was so overcome by shock and disbelief in the moment that she was not capable of insisting on seeing her daughter one last time. Not only this but she was also raised to follow the rules and not question people of authority, so when the officers in charge at the scene told her no (for whatever reason), she could not find her voice. She likely had a trauma response in that moment where everything inside of her went into shock and froze up—even her words. Also, being somewhat shy and introverted, she didn't ask or insist on getting her way. With such devastation all around her, how could she? However, now, whenever she sees a law enforcement official, or especially paramedics, cold fear runs down her spine, and she feels short of breath. Her story further illustrates what van der Kolk illuminates about going through such terrible things:

> *We have learned that trauma is not just an event that took place sometime in the past; it is also the imprint left by that experience on mind, brain, and body. This imprint has ongoing consequences for how the human organism manages to survive in the present. Trauma results in a fundamental reorganization of the way the mind and brain manage perceptions. It changes not only how we think and what we think about, but also our very capacity to think. (Bessel van der Kolk, The Body Keeps the Score: Brain, Mind, and Body in the Healing of Trauma)*

Because our capacity to even think has been upended by our losses, it's important that we begin somewhere to try and get a small foothold on what's happened. Hot spots may be a good place to start. If this process is too overwhelming, I suggest taking this section to a trusted leader and asking them to walk with you through the process. Also, please remember that this is a book about post-traumatic growth, NOT about comprehensive trauma treatment. There is much work to do for some of us who need more in-depth trauma work. This is only a place to begin.

Working with hot spots like these can be done by simply starting with what's signaling the dread or "heat" of what happened, identifying what was missing or needed at the time, and then working to find specific ways to empower yourself now and plan for future situations. This is essentially a cope-ahead plan for future catastrophes and a way to self-soothe in the face of things that signal our past traumas and lock us up.

I will walk you through what answers might look like, using Lauren's example from above. Begin by asking yourself the following questions:

What things or places carry scary, bad, or uncomfortable memories? One way to recognize these places or things is that you are struck with intense emotion when you remember, see, or think about them. Another way is to notice your urge to avoid these things and places.

- Paramedics

- Police officers

What did I need then? These could be things you wish you had that could've helped you manage what was happening.

- More time to think about what was happening

- To touch and see my daughter

- To use my voice

- To insist on what I need from people of authority

What can I do now to help myself? One way to come up with these is to try accessing specific skills or tools you've learned since the difficult event or even that you've learned from this book. For example:

When I see a police officer or ambulance, or when I feel cold fear, I can take a moment to do four-square breathing. I can imagine a four-sided square in my mind's eye and then slowly breathe in and out in sequence with the square.

I can place my hand over my heart as a signal of my love for my daughter and for myself. This will help me remember to go easy on myself and not rush past what is happening.

I can call a trusted friend to help ground me where I am and validate my struggle.

I can remember that most police officers and paramedics do good work and are just following the protocols that have been laid out for them by their management. Just like when I go to work and follow the procedures of my employer, they are doing their jobs.

I can practice new situations (maybe small at first) of speaking up and using my voice in front of others when normally I might shy away.

Catch and hug the family members I still have near me, and take a few seconds to be present and feel them in my arms as much as possible each day.

Spend time reading stories about police officers and para- medics who get it right for other families.

Investigate the science of forgiveness and consider the pros and cons of such a gesture.

Working Through Our Hot Spots

While working through your hot spots, you may find that you have dozens of events that hurt you during your process of loss. Go through the three questions we outlined earlier and then complete a to-do list of things you can begin working on now and in the days to come. If your to-do-now list from each hot spot topic contains the same or similar things like "hug my family members more often" or "speak up even if it makes me uncomfortable," this is a signal to prioritize that item. You have revealed your own patterns to yourself and now have the power to change this when you're ready.

If changing the patterns that emerge seems too daunting, start small. For instance, to a naturally shy person, speaking up more often may feel like too much. That is OK. Instead, try letting two of your closest friends or family members know you are practicing being more assertive. Invite them to be patient with you in the coming days as you try your new skill of speak- ing up about small things. Then, give it a try by perhaps trying these things:

- Sending back food you don't like at a restaurant

- Saying no to people you usually say yes to

- Sticking with your opinion in a debate

As you work through your hot spots using your to-do-now list, you will build a "muscle" for new patterns that are more in line with what you want in life. Warning: This will be painful. You won't want to keep at it. It will be easier to avoid it. Why? Because this was a place of tension, friction, and unusual agony amidst the swirling mess of your personal tragedy. In short, it hurts like hell to address these things. The way physical muscles grow is the same way we grow and change. We feel pressure from the exertion of life's hurdles, we get torn apart as we make our way through them, and all of our current capacities are challenged beyond what we think we can bear. And we are right! These are things we're not equipped to handle, *and* in handling them, we become stronger, more confident people. Under a heavy load, our abilities get stronger, so stay with it. The way to learn how to do great things is to effectively handle hard things that matter in smaller portions.

This chapter provided a variety of tools to help you develop a personalized list of self-care practices. Relinquishing guilt, creating margin, using PLEASE and Allow Skills, and creating a go-to list of Instant Mood Shifters will anchor you in times of loss and grief. We can learn a lot from our furry friends, who keep us company, soothe us, and are living demonstrations of how to be mindful and stay present in the moment. If you're in a heavy period of grief, I've shared grounding exercises and additional coping strategies to keep you moving forward. Finally, the section on hot spots offers you the opportunity to identify the traumas that happened during your loss. Self-care doesn't have to be costly or time-consuming, just intentional.

The tools in the next chapter will help you start working on the true story of your sadness, which is your story of loss. Understanding what need that loss was filling for you will allow you to find what remains and how to take your next steps.

Chapter 4

Lost and Found

"Every act of creation is first an act of destruction."

—PABLO PICASSO

HARD THINGS MATTER

The Greeks have a name for situations that undo us: *steno-choria*, a narrow place of crushing. Perhaps life and all the *stenochoria* it has for us transforms us into something greater. There's nothing I know more difficult or crushing than the experience of deep loss. Perhaps people go through hard times, difficult, crushing experiences, and harrowing episodes, and come out on the other end changed, transformed, and better for it.

But many of us want to avoid things that crush us. And for good reason—they're often terrible experiences! But what if we *need* them? When life goes well, we rarely have to do hard things, so we're kept from building the skillset or muscles for doing so. Like our physical muscles, which only get stronger by using them, the muscle of handling hard things grows only by *handling* hard things. By going through our loss and grief now, we learn how to manage not only future loss but future difficulties, and we grow as people. By being pressed, we learn what it feels like and how to endure pressure. When we are crushed, we learn how to adapt, to re-shape ourselves.

For instance, childbirth is dramatic for both mother and child. But the exacting work of delivering a baby vaginally has enormous benefits for both mom and child and is exactly what that baby needs to face the world outside the safety and protection of the mother's womb.[2]

Babies get much needed maternal bacteria through vaginal birth (rather than cesarean section), which inoculates them from later health problems; their lungs get a good squeezing, which reduces the risk of newborn breathing problems; and their overall risk of childhood asthma and obesity are drastically reduced as well. Afterward, mom and baby get up and around quicker, mom tends to breastfeed more quickly and for a longer period of time (which is great for both her and the baby), and future fertility is easier to guarantee for mom. All from the painful experience of being born!

While I'm not trying to say which type of birth is better (trust me there are lots of benefits to C-sections as well), I am saying that pain has a purpose. And when we let it do its important work, it can have far-reaching benefits.

---

2 "WHO Recommendations Non-Clinical Interventions to Reduce Unnecessary Caesarean Sections," Geneva: World Health Organization, 2018. apps.who.int/iris/bitstream/handle/10665/275377/9789241550338-eng.pdf

---

Ray Dalio says, "Every time you confront something painful, you are at a potentially important juncture in your life—you have the opportunity to choose healthy and painful truth or unhealthy but comfortable delusion."

What makes this statement so hard is that "healthy and painful truth" does not sound nearly as good as comfortable delusion. So first, let's look at our goals. To be happy or not?

To be happy, all I'd need to do is buy a pineapple pizza and a sleeve of Oreos; lie in my bed and watch twelve hours of Netflix with my best friend; laugh and talk; roll over at the end of the day and sleep well; wake up and do it all over again. This would indeed make me happy. But this type of happiness (while fun) lacks the up-close experiences that can lead us to *real* happiness.

What studies have found (thanks, Harvard)[3] is that lasting happiness comes from doing what we're good at, helping others, facing and overcoming challenges, and through a warm, deep connection with others. I'd take it one step further and add that discovering what we were created to do is also a path to happiness. And often, grief and loss lead us to that discovery. Brushing up against difficulties, learning how to handle them, and discovering what we are made of can lead us to make deep, lasting connections with ourselves and with others along the journey. That is happiness. But that also comes with the price

---

3   Mineo, Liz. "Good genes are nice, but joy is better," *Harvard Gazette*. Harvard Public Affairs & Communications, April 11, 2017. https://news.harvard.edu/gazette/story/2017/04/over-nearly-80-years-harvard-study-has-been-showing-how-to-live-a-healthy-and-happy-life/.

WHEN GRIEF IS GOOD

tag of learning to accept healthy, painful truths. For instance, I cannot gain happiness by avoiding my pain. I cannot find the relationships I long for by being online all day. I will not grow unless I can become somewhat comfortable with growing pains. Everything we need to make us who we long to be is on the other side of doing the things we fear.

We have to make sure we are engaging in life. Hard life. Taking it on. Getting thrown down by it, sizing it up, and coming back for another round. When we face hard times, even if we do it feeling like cowards, failures, and imposters, there's something about it that makes us better. Stronger. Able to handle more. To grow. To feel fulfilled.

Glennon Doyle writes, "You are not supposed to be happy all the time. Life hurts and it's hard. Not because you're doing it wrong, but because it hurts for everybody. Don't avoid the pain. You need it. It's meant for you. Be still with it, let it come, let it go, let it leave you with the fuel you'll burn to get your work done on this earth."

It turns out that in handling hard things, with the proper tools and support, we grow more capable, resilient, and confident. It's like a weightlifter at the gym. As she strains to lift the barbell, the muscles of her arms develop multiple tiny tears and shreds as they are pressed over and over again to lift the weights. The tearing is a result of the pressure and stress on the muscle. Once the athlete goes home to rest, the body heals these tears by repairing them with more tissue. The result: bigger, stronger muscles! The heavier the load you face, the stronger you become.

Personal growth, internal strength, and increased capacity all happen when we are placed under pressure, face challenges, and are forced to grow the muscles of emotional endurance.

We become like life-athletes with a high capacity to do hard things. And that sometimes feels good. In fact, it might even feel a lot like success and confidence down the line, after the dust has cleared. Once we grow the confidence and strength it takes to do hard things, happiness and confidence *within ourselves* is a natural by-product.

Please note: when we develop a high tolerance for life's pain, it can mean different things to different people. While one person may experience a sense of mastery and confidence upon summiting the top of their troubles and facing into their challenges, for others, this might be a false or missing summit in their own loss response. They may have farther to go. To survive and overcome an adverse experience is really surviving a million little and big, very difficult things, over a long period of time. Many of us have been injured deeply along the way.

During hard times, people may experience any range of trauma, neglect, abuse, physical harm, shunning, rejection, or other forms of punishment and humiliation. Yes, they have survived, but what that literally means is they made it out alive. It does not mean they are well. Whatever they are dealing with—job loss, divorce, heartbreak, death, major illness, betrayal, deployment, riots—likely left some bruises. Rather than die a "death by a thousand cuts" as Taylor Swift sings about, let's work on managing expectations during this time. It's quite normal to be debilitated for a time by the difficulties of life. Did you know that? In fact,

- some of us will need specific, targeted therapeutic treatments for the traumas we've endured, while others may also need ongoing supportive counseling or an intensive retreat.

- some may have a clinical diagnosis of PTSD or complex PTSD and need not only various forms of treatment and therapy but might also be well-served by an assistive therapy pet, a support group, or by reading about people who overcame their particular struggle.

- some will be evaluated by a physician and given appropriate medication and/or accommodations at work.

Wherever you find yourself, let the next parts of this chapter help you navigate through a gentle off-loading process, so your grief doesn't build up and become explosive or overwhelming.

IDENTIFYING THE LOSS

Before we move on to the assignment, a word on the meaning of our losses. When we endure the puncture wounds of loss, it's like a bite from one mouth with many teeth. In losing one thing, we often lose several associated things as well. Here are some examples of compounded loss because of a single event:

Death of a Loved One

There is not one comprehensive list that can cover everything actually lost when someone dies. Because our relationships are so different, and people are so different, it's impossible to identify exactly what one loses when someone dies. For instance, for one family, the death of a mother can carry

heartache because she was so beloved for her warmth, caring, attention and intimate connection with each family member. But for another family, the death of the matriarch might be a relief. Some mothers (and fathers) leave such a legacy of pain and chaos that their death actually allows family members to finally exhale once they're gone. Often, it's easier to address and heal these difficult entanglements after the parent is deceased. For those family members, dealing with losing a parent while also grappling with the fallout wrought by that parent is a double-whammy and complex path of grieving.

Certainly, their age and the way a person died carries weight as we identify the associated losses. To lose a child, for instance, carries the eternal sting of a death that was unwelcome in the first place, out of step with time, thief-like, and most unfair. Death came to snatch our tenderling, and all that's left is the possibility of what could've been, what should've been. People who lose a child often cite feeling like there's been a death of all their dreams, a sense of being stolen from, and victimhood for a life cut short.

As an example, my husband lost his older brother Keith, and his dad, in 2020, only six months apart. The timing and means of death left such an impact. Keith, a seasoned police officer in his late fifties, died from suicide, while his dad, Jack, was nearly ninety and died rather normally from cancer. Keith's death carried so many unanswered questions, and everything about it felt like the "wrong way to die." But Jack's death felt like what we might call "the right way to die."

When someone dies, we don't just lose a person; we also lose a part of ourselves. Other losses that accompany a loved one's death may include how we felt when we were around them, the loss of their role in our life (as a confidant, compan-

ion, lover, friend, family member, neighbor), and the loss of our role in *their* life. My husband lost his role as brother and son when his brother and dad died.

We also lose their everyday presence, and must deal with changes to our routine, our stability, our sense of security, perhaps even our physical location. Conversely, for caretakers of loved ones suffering from a long illness, they may feel relief that their loved one is finally at peace and pain-free. Perhaps their death allows more freedom—from routine, physical location, financial obligations, or the demands of caretaking; only you know the answers to identifying what you've lost. I will provide more guidance in this chapter to help you gain clarity and articulate it plainly.

Divorce

When we go through divorce, we not only lose our companionship with a spouse but we often lose where we live, our schedules, part of our money, and the experience of having another parent to help with the kids. Divorce can also mean the loss of treasured extended family members, our identity as a married couple, holiday family traditions, and sometimes the loss of entire social groups and longtime friendships. If you are the parent who is believed to be *at fault* for the crumbling of the marriage for whatever reason, or if you're just the *one who filed*, beware of the toll this might also take on the relationship with your kids.

Many a parent has lost the favor of one or more of their children in the wake of the bulldozer of divorce and family court. Parents who find themselves as the villain are also alienated and treated as lesser or adversarial beings by the rest of the

family. There's often a crumbling of shared trust between this parent and child. Treasured times together become fewer, and the affectionate bond between them may dwindle as sides are drawn up and wounds are licked. Family alliances, cut-offs, estrangements, and grudges often come into play during the end of a marriage, and the onslaught of multiple losses begins to pile up.

Betrayal by a Spouse

When one spouse faces the devastation of their partner's choices—like infidelity, sexual addiction, financial betrayal, secretive behaviors, and other disloyalties—they typically experience shock, disbelief, and a feeling of being core-shaken. Things like safety, predictability, trust, and expectations are altered. Often the most destabilizing of traumas, a partner's betrayal not only affects a person's future but it calls all of their past into question as well. The couple's losses are many and varied. I lean on a trusted resource when I share this perspective from Affair Recovery, founded by Rick and Stephanie Reynolds, in the wake of their own story of betrayal.

> *Betrayal trauma shatters the couple's story, and makes the betrayed question every memory with the unfaithful as a lie. Accepting that Marriage 1.0 is over is hard, forgiving and accepting brokenness with hope of renewal in Marriage 2.0 is even harder. It requires hard work, and a community of those going through affair recovery together. Most of all, the betrayed who*

commits to reconciliation feels "isolated" from her family and friends because until you have been there and been through it, most people would never contemplate doing it or getting it. "You should leave him," or "I would never put up with that." Simply put, most people would not do affair recovery work. Shame, guilt, self-doubt are difficult for most to live with and it takes a few seasons to go through each phase of recovery. Infidelity is the keeping of secrets. Hurt people hide.

Job Loss

Facing a downturn or failure in our careers can be particularly tough. Many don't view losing or leaving a job as something that needs to be grieved. And true enough, losing one's job may not seem the same as losing a loved one. But they can feel similar. When we lose or leave a job, not only are we faced with the absence of our monthly paycheck but also with losing our coworkers, friends, and a familiar, daily schedule. To some, their job was their whole life. It was the source of their meaning, purpose, connection, achievement, celebrations, and identity. This is why we see spikes in the rates of suicide amongst (mostly) men who are laid off or fired, lose their business, or are facing retirement. Very dedicated and conscientious, these professionals have been providing for their family and themselves through their careers, and now, all of it is gone. When any one of us is highly identified with our job, the resultant damage from being displaced is often debilitating.

Natural Disasters

Those who have made it through an earthquake, hurricane, avalanche, flood, wildfire, or other episodes of drastic, traumatic natural disasters, are usually quite altered by the incident, and often never again return to their prior ways of thinking or feeling. Not only is their life, family, and well-being toppled but often their home, car, and/or job may be destroyed as well. Sometimes entire neighborhoods and familiar places are suddenly leveled by an angry act of Mother Nature. In her path, many victims must survey not only the damage wrought in their own life but also that of those in proximity.

Neighbors may watch another's house burn, see their car carried away, watch nearby fields flood, or see a local's store crushed. Tornados and flash floods typically leave a host of victims in their path. People who walk away from natural disasters can still remark, months and years later, that there's nowhere that feels safe for them. Even when viable help is made ready, there's no getting away from the shock and blow of the sting. If you've ever worked in a Red Cross encampment, practical help like food, bedding, and shelter is very much needed. However, the victims of these disasters also tend to look like the walking dead, both immediately after the ordeal and for quite some time to come.

It's not unusual to hear that survivors experience changes in their sleep/wake cycles, thought patterns, body functions, sense of safety, and more. It's quite common for survivors to have physical maladies, including migraines, indigestion, various physical pains, nightmares, and ongoing transient health conditions. Additionally, surviving traumatic natural events can give rise to poor work and school performance and cause the emergence of psychiatric disorders. Some may develop agitated or aggressive behaviors, which can erode interpersonal relationships. And it appears that the younger the age during the traumatic event, the more susceptible the victim is to the effects of the trauma. With little ability to naturally protect oneself and immature brain development, children fare the worst in these types of situations.[4]

Pandemics and World Events

World events such as pandemics, political unrest, unstable government, diaspora (the dispersion of people from their homeland), immigration, and refugee situations can all lead to trauma, grief, and loss. At the writing of this text, millions have perished and the losses from COVID-19 are still growing. No part of everyday life is untouched. Humans have faced these losses on all major fronts: physical, financial, emotional, spiritual, political, and educational. This pandemic has been such a monumental event that as a society, we have even begun marking time by it, "Before COVID" (BC) and "After COVID" (AC). COVID-19 has been a worldwide traumatic event with thousands of spin-off traumas left in its wake.

---

4 "Behavioral Health Conditions in Children and Youth Exposed to Natural Disasters," *Disaster Technical Assistance Center Supplemental Research Bulletin.* Substance Abuse and Mental Health Services Administration, September, 2018. https://www.samhsa.gov/sites/default/files/srb-childrenyouth-8-22-18.pdf.

Survivors of Life-Threatening Illnesses

A person who survives a devastating illness can be thought of like a house that's been gutted and needs to be rebuilt from the ground up. Most, if not all, of the original structure must be assessed, deconstructed, and reassembled. Indeed, life after a traumatic illness will look quite different for the survivor. Body parts, systems, mental health, and physical function have likely all been impacted and may not run the same way, now or maybe ever again. The rebooting process can take months or years. Physical function, mental agility, optimism about the future, and more must be considered when counting the losses from a complex medical condition.

Collateral Losses

I am providing a table full of topics in the Appendix so you can locate yourself depending on the type of loss you're experiencing.

Of course, I can't outline every single kind of loss, but my hope is that these examples illustrate the ripple effect one loss can have and prompt you to find and identify the effects of loss in your own life. It's also possible that you grieve a loss even when you're moving on to something potentially positive. Whether it was your choice to move on or retire, or you initiated the divorce, there's still value in completing the assignment that follows.

LOST AND FOUND ASSIGNMENT

This particular tool moves you through a three-part processing of your loss by looking at what you lost, what it meant to you, what you still have in your life, and what you can then do with that information.

Then, you will identify what remains and next steps to take. Even if you feel you already know, being able to label it moves you into a better understanding of how to get this need met.

Begin by defining specifically what you lost because of the event(s) that took place. I'll share an example of a loss in my life, with a Lost and Found assignment I partially completed for myself.

Who/What Did I Lose?

First, I identified the specific loss:

I lost Colin, our son's best friend. He lived with us while he and my son were going to college together. He was eighteen years old and died suddenly in an accident near our house. I called Colin my "bonus kid." He was like my third son. I was his "House Mom." He called my husband and me "Mom and Dad" multiple times a day and was an instant member of our family.

Then, I elaborated about what I lost:

My eldest son had just moved away to college the year before. When Colin moved in, it felt like his presence soothed the part of my heart that missed having both my boys home with me. When Colin arrived, there were two boys in the house again! It was wonderful to have him with us, especially because he was such a warm and open kid. He provided a lot of happiness for my younger son, and they had fun around the house together. I was happy for my son and myself; having the two boys in the house was comforting, and Colin's presence brought joy and excitement every day to our home. My son lost his best friend in a traumatic way, and I had to see, feel, hear, and experience the trauma. I lost my sense of safety in the world for a time. We loved him deeply and were devastated on every level when we were notified of his death. It was unbelievable.

Before Colin's death, I thought that when anybody came and went from my house—be it friends or family or neighbors—they would inherently be safe wherever they went next. My sense of safety was fractured when he died. *The streets in my neighborhood aren't even safe anymore. Anything can happen at any time. My kids or my husband or myself or my neighbors could leave their house and be hit and killed by a car.* I had a strong sense of vulnerability, as if I was waiting for the next bad thing to happen, and as if the whole world was unsafe. I also lost the role of being a mentor to Colin because he would talk to me about his life, struggles, his girlfriend in Minnesota, his college major, about getting a job, and about his dreams. I enjoyed that role because he was easy to talk to, and I felt like I was contributing to the greater good of a bright young life.

The other thing that hit hard was the reality of his age (eighteen years old) and the impermanence of this life for all of us. I had to grapple with my own expectations about how long a life *should* be. I was very spun out by the fact that we might not all be given our full life span to live. Apparently, an average life expectancy of eighty-five years comes with no guarantees or warranties, expressed or implied. I also had to excavate the fantasy that all young people should never be subjected to mayhem, difficulties, or death. I thought a young person *should be* exempt from all of this, and so for a time, I lost my bearings in the structure and order of things that I had grown accustomed to.

You can complete this assignment by writing out entire sentences like I did or in bullet form, like this:

I lost Colin.

- My "bonus" kid

- Someone who called me "Mom"

- My third son

- My son, Brandon's best friend

- My sense of safety in the world

- My role as a mentor

- My faith, for a period of time

What Remains?

The next part is to ask yourself *What do I still have, even though I lost all these things?* Look at what remains that you can touch and connect with. Where do you feel empowered or have agency? What could you do? What do you have some say about? What can you continue on with?

For me, I still had

- Kayla (Colin's sister);

- Sebastian, Dimitri, Tyler, and the other kids from back home (Brandon's other friends);

- this one moment; and

- quite thankfully, my own children, Jordan, Brandon, and Zach, and my husband Darin.

Here's how I wrote about this lost and found experience in long-form.

One of the things that was left for me was Colin's older sister, Kayla. (She was five years older than Colin, and she felt like an extension of our family. She had recently moved to be near Colin. She's a lovely soul.)

Also, I still had the presence of my son's other friends. He had three close friends, and I always enjoyed when they came over. Bringing friendships together had always made me feel very satisfied and content as a parent. To see my children's friends enjoying our home, talking, and hanging out made me feel that my home was a nurturing space for them. And my home could continue to be a safe space for them. I could focus on, connect with, and experience this process with Brandon and his other friends.

Even though my sense of safety in the world was gone, when I did this exercise, I saw that I still had the present moment. I realized that all thoughts about whether I was safe or unsafe were about my fear of the future, about something that may or may not happen, catastrophes that might befall me or someone I love, or threats to my life or someone else's life. And they were mostly based in fear about the future. I didn't have a crystal ball or a magic wand to make sure that the future was going to be OK, but I had that moment I was in right then. I could bring my attention and my focus to that moment in time and release what I couldn't control. If I was able to live more in the moment, with intention, that could give me a sense of traction with what was still being given to me.

What also remained for me were my own children. My gratitude that my own three children were still safe and sound in that moment meant I felt such a rush of love, care, and a desire to protect them as never before. Because my children still remained, I could deepen into those relationships. I could call them. I could set intentions around being closer to them in life.

What Can I Do Next?

As an outcome of the first two steps, you may discover that action steps naturally open up for you. You want to create an action with the things that still remain.

For me, that meant the following, for example:

1. Prioritizing my kids' friends when they come over.

Sit and listen to them, remember their birthdays, check in on how they're doing, celebrate with them, perhaps mentor them if that's a possibility.

2. Practicing mindfulness toward driving and motorcycles.

The driver that killed Colin was distracted when she hit him. I still have control over this present moment and my own driving. Even though Colin was killed in a motorcycle accident, I am often a driver in traffic where there are motorcycles around me. My next step is to increase my awareness while I drive, stop multitasking, and be present to other people around me. I can improve my driving skills and increase my caution so I avoid inadvertently causing an accident. I have power in my life to make sure I'm driving effectively and skillfully and am as present as possible.

3. Reaching out to Colin's sister and maintaining that connection.

We have a big, shared experience of losing Colin, and maintaining that relationship feels vital.

4. Not missing out on a hug.

I was the last one to see Colin as he was putting on his gear to get on his bike. I was on a phone call for work when I saw him in the front yard. Normally we would hug, and I'd say something like "I love you, honey. Have a good night at work," or "See you tomorrow." But that day, I didn't do it because I was working. Instead, I did a quick wave with my headphones in. Something I can prioritize now is getting hugs from people in the moment (this has an even more critical meaning in the socially distanced time of COVID-19). So, my next step is to prioritize hugs, to put down what I'm doing, and enter into that loving space with the people in my life.

Protective Factors and Risk Factors

Oftentimes it's only when we consider and list what remains that we realize we have a community or that we have people willing to help. Or that we still have our own health. We have the support to help us go through hard times and bounce back better.

When times are hard, psychology refers to the things we do, believe, have, or engage in that protect us from greater harm as *protective factors*. Protective factors protect us from risks like homelessness, drug or alcohol abuse, or abusive relationships. These factors essentially insulate us against the worst things in life.

Protective factors wrap around us and help us move on our way. It's important to identify what has been lost because when you lose your job, you may lose the protective factors the job provided, like your friend group. Not only are your finances threatened but the very community who would pick you up and cheer you on from this loss is no longer readily available. You are isolated from them and therefore more at risk in your life. Isolation, loneliness, and being cut off from your community can easily drop you into a worse place because you're no longer protected by those things that cushioned you.

Making a list of protective factors that remain counterbalances the collateral losses you've experienced due to your central loss. This list helps you see that you're richer than you think, and that while your loss is real and weighty, you have protective factors to lean on.

Protective factors may include the following:

- Positive attitudes, values, or beliefs

- Conflict resolution skills

- Good mental, physical, spiritual, and emotional health

- Positive self-esteem

- Success at school

- Good parenting skills

- Parental supervision

- Strong social supports

- Community engagement

- Problem-solving skills

- Positive adult role models

- Coaches and mentors

- Healthy prenatal and early childhood development

- Participation in traditional healing and cultural activities

- Supportive peer group/friends

- Steady employment

- Stable housing

- Availability of services (social, recreational, cultural, etc.)

In turn, risk factors—the antithesis of protective factors— put an individual and community at greater risk of failure and decay. Here are some examples:

- Negative attitudes, values, or beliefs

- Low self-esteem

- Drug, alcohol, or solvent abuse

- Poverty

- Children of parents in conflict with the law

- Homelessness

- Presence of neighborhood crime

- Early and repeated antisocial behavior

- Lack of positive role models

- Children who witness violence

- Lack of services (social, recreational, cultural, etc.)

- Unemployment/underemployment

- Family distress

- Racism

- Mental or physical illness

- Low literacy

- Leaving institutional/government care (hospital, foster care, correctional facility, etc.)

- Family violence

When you look at protective factors, you may discover that you have more than you realize. If you have a close community of friends and family, it's quite possible that you can lean on them when you go through something like a death or divorce. They may bring meals, drive your children to school, or come over and help clean the house. They may show up late at night when you're lonely. When your community helps you in hard times, they become protectors. Imagine what life would be like if you didn't have help driving your children to school, or someone making sure you had some food if your house was in total disarray, or if you didn't have anybody to talk to. When we lost Colin, our community jumped into action. We were so amazed! We had only been house parents to him, but some of them instinctively knew we would ache alongside Colin's family and Brandon, so they'd quietly drop meals at our door and call to check on us.

When you are low on protective factors, you risk falling prey to things like mental illness, thoughts of suicide, severe depression, homelessness, drug and alcohol abuse, and other ineffective, unhealthy ways of dealing with stress. When you have protective factors, the likelihood you will develop more resilience—the ability to not just bounce back from a hard time, but to bounce forward—increases.

When your children have a community around them, friends show up to take them to school on time or help them with their homework while their dad and mom are going through a divorce. They're more likely to pass their classes and maybe even get scholarships, get into a school of their choice, and feel a sense of success and esteem despite the chaos and disruption they may feel at home. When nobody can take them to school, or they have a long bus ride, or they're being bullied and nobody notices, they risk descending into a life of trauma, chaos, and frustration.

These are examples of things that can come along and derail your children and even predispose them to mental illness, to becoming victims in life, or making poor life choices.

I believe my children were prevented from further suffering and worse outcomes because of the loving community that surrounded us.

YOUR LOST AND FOUND

This exercise works for all types of grief. It's helpful to know what you've lost so you can get clear about where you are emotionally and better understand why you're thinking and feeling the way you are. When we know that what we're experiencing is normal, it's easier to manage. And you need things that are "easy" right now as often as you can get them. For larger losses, it might take a few times going through the exercise before feeling any sense of relief. For perceived "smaller" losses, it may be more of a mental exercise that helps you shift your mindset. You can ask the questions for each of the different losses you have or are currently experiencing.

1. What have I lost?

2. What remains?

3. Next steps?

4. What protective factors do I have?

Repeat the Lost and Found exercise as many times as you need to in order to move into understanding the various losses you may be experiencing and the impact they've had or are having on your life.

FROM *STENOCHORIA* TO STRENGTH

Labeling what you lost and then identifying your remaining protective factors at this stage is important, so you can lean on what you have as you grieve through what you've lost. You may feel like you are in *stenochoria*, that narrow place of crushing. But remember, you're building muscle and learning how to re-shape yourself into something greater. There is no better time to examine how you think about the world, about others, and about yourself.

When we're able to see that our experience was a compounded set of difficulties, we can give ourselves permission to dig in a little and slow down to look at each one. By acknowledging the complex nature of the loss and then seeing what we *still* have with us, we can take specific, small steps to help ourselves and balance the story.

In the next chapter, you get to say goodbye to the beliefs that are keeping you stuck in your grief.

Chapter 5

Resetting Our Expectations

"The cave you fear to enter holds the treasure you seek."

—JOSEPH CAMPBELL

We recently visited a beautiful part of Northern California known as the Napa Valley. Napa Valley is home to some of the world's finest wines. The grapes grown in this valley are on par with those in Bordeaux and Burgundy, France. The wines produced by this tiny area of the country have won awards and are highly sought after, and they're sold for hundreds of dollars per ounce.

Upon touring one of the wineries, we learned about the special barrels the wine is stored in, about the temperature, and how corks are made. We learned about the aging process, the harvest, and the area's weather patterns that all come together to make the wines of Napa so famous. Everything can impact a good "vintage," including the soil and weather conditions, and the time of harvest. And forest fires can certainly have an impact on the grapes. But I was especially intrigued to learn that a drought can *increase the flavor* of a grape, leading to an excellent year of wine. So when a vineyard is placed under stress and pressure and denied what it appears to need, it can produce some rich benefits.

People are like this too. Have you ever met someone like that? The more they go through, the better they get. Though life has thrown them some curveballs, they still stand up, swing their bat, and run the bases, getting stronger and stronger each time. My friend and colleague Lori Jean Glass is like this.

Born in West Virginia and raised in the national parks, hers was a chaotic and dark existence from the beginning. At only three years old, she watched her father drown in the Potomac River and went home with her mother, who proceeded to drown her sorrows in a daily bottle of vodka. Ducking for cover from a family whose core was flawed from the earliest moments, Lori Jean learned early to care not only for herself but also for her debilitated mother. To keep her mother from drinking more, she dumped bottles of alcohol down the drain and filled them with water, knowing she would get beaten for it. She became a caregiver (as many children must) for her mom. Relying on friends' parents to shelter her after her mother burned their house down, the drought in her life continued. She would eventually bury her mom, who committed suicide when Lori was only seventeen.

Parentless and lost, she embarked on adulthood and tried to pass as an average person from a regular family. She looked the part on the outside, attractive, successful, and confident as the number one salesperson for Loreal. But under the surface, a gaping hole of broken attachments, loss, and trauma stood ready to consume her. As a little girl, she often fantasized about how wonderful her family could be with the safe, loving arms of her mom and dad around her, and all of them in a happy home. But in reality, she lived in a perpetual state of outrunning her past, flanked by loneliness, and searching for safety in her present. Caught in a feedback loop of fear and abandonment, she came to believe that a burning, anxious drive to survive was the only way to live.

Eventually, it became too much for her. After becoming a mom of two young sons while struggling to figure out how to navigate healthy relationships, she was pushed into a life of pain (like her mom) and to the brink of suicide. Another failed relationship and the utter end of her coping skills, plus years of untreated developmental trauma and loss, had leveled her. Stuck in old survival patterns from her childhood, she faced life in her late thirties like a little girl, lost and with no way home. Hopelessly in search of her dad in the face of every man she met, life certainly had no happy ending for her.

Just minutes before she would've taken her own life, an unexpected call from a therapist brought her back to her senses. She realized she could either fall victim to the same demons that haunted her family, or she could take a different path: she could help herself find a new way and then help other people do the same thing.

Armed with the knowledge she gained from her healing journey, an understanding of the wounds she had endured, a spitfire determination to survive, and a keen sense of how to relate to others, she began putting together a comprehensive curriculum aimed at pulling people from the wreckage of their own lives. She instinctively knew that if people were going to stand up and take control of their lives, they would have to learn how to pivot from fantasy to reality, from their childhood survival patterns into healthy adults, just like she had. She took all her grief and loss and made it *good*, not just for herself, but for others too.

Pulling from the hundreds of hours she spent in therapy, dozens of personal failures and triumphs, thousands of hours of study and research, she combined the best therapy and recovery traditions into one overarching application and called it Pivot. Lori Jean brought Pivot to life based on developmental psychology and delivered it in the setting of coaching and retreats (accessible to all, to reduce the stigma of seeking care). Years later, and tested in a clinical setting, Pivot has helped thousands of people find their healthy adult selves. Her work at the Glass House and across the country has caused her to be sought out by celebrities, industry leaders, renowned families, and individuals across every walk of life.

Along the way, just like Lori Jean had to, we must all come to grips with the conflict between how we thought life was going to be and how it *actually* turns out. In the face of significant loss, we must learn to reset our expectations and amend our belief system.

We all have a belief system about ourselves, about others, and about how the world works. This internal guidance system has been developed throughout our life as we've had experiences, made choices, seen consequences, and been in relationships. In short, we've developed a handbook for how we believe life is, how it should go, and what should and should not be happening in our life.

It's only natural that when we experience the life-altering process of loss, we take out this internal rule book about life and how the world works because I can guarantee you that some of our beliefs about ourselves and others have been violated. We may have believed things were one way, and this new loss has shown us that things are not that way. Our hope of how things have always gone in the past and how we thought our life would play out have been uprooted by our recent devastation. And when our experiences and losses have been especially traumatic, specialists say we actually "lose our innocence" about life.

FIND YOUR FOOTING IN THE WAKE OF LOSS

You've begun to recalibrate your expectations, learned that things are indeed difficult and messy and that life is more of an off-road experience than a tidy straight line. But you've also learned it can lead to a deep sense of confidence and mastery. Now, we need to clarify what you want. I doubt that happiness is your goal right now. Maybe your goal is to "try and get back to normal" or "find my center" or just to "get out of bed." This chapter gets underneath the ineffective thought patterns that no longer serve you in the aftermath of your sorrow and loss. By completing this assignment, you begin to shed the thoughts that are keeping you stuck. A reminder here: you are not your thoughts. Your thoughts exist because you grew up listening to people talk in a certain way. Your malleable mind absorbed those voices, and now they're on repeat every day, all the time, automatically. It's natural to internalize our caretakers' voices so much that they become our own thoughts. But these tapes in our heads are not permanent, can be changed, and are rarely based on facts. They're just a script we were handed, and we can re-write that script. Now may be the perfect time to do that. In essence, going through loss is a good time to examine how we think about the world, about others, and about ourselves.

This chapter invites you to review your current rule book and see what kind of amendments or updates you can make to the machine of your mind. As you develop a new belief system, you can find new ways of thinking that can lead you to much relief.

As I've shared in previous chapters, I have survived multiple losses. I've partially completed this assignment as an example.

Exercise—Reviewing Your Current Rule Book

First, we begin by identifying the beliefs that have been violated or are no longer true in the wake of loss. I'll share examples of three beliefs that were upended through my loss.

Everything always works out.

I used to have a fairytale belief, from the little girl living inside me, that *everything always works out. Everything will be OK. We'll get to have the Hollywood ending.*

If I do good, I will receive good.

I used to believe that *bad things should not happen to me because I've been a good person. If people are good, good things should happen to them.* In myth-busting that belief, I realized I thought life was very transactional, when in fact, it is not.

Other people should believe and act the same way I do.

We're all comfortable with those people in our lives who mirror our values. We're the most at ease with people who are like us. And a lot of us are uncomfortable with people who have different beliefs, points of view, colors of skin, or ways of living. That creates tension as we try to reconcile their value system with our own. When I was unflinchingly honest with myself, the reason behind my belief that *other people should believe and act the way I do* was that it made me uncomfortable when they didn't. I was so uncomfortable with people being different from me that I also set out to try and change them, in both subtle and not so subtle ways.

I had to examine these beliefs and let them go because grief showed me that these beliefs were not serving me well. First, they weren't true. But more importantly, by continuing to hold the limiting belief, I was keeping myself stuck and hurting the people around me. My belief system was out of sync with my reality. I had to move into a new belief system; I replaced my old beliefs with new ones as described here.

Old Belief—Everything Always Works Out

I was able to identify that not only did I have to amend my narrative about life, others, and myself but I also had to accept the new narrative, not just state it from a cerebral headspace. My new belief was that *not everything works out, but most of it does.* I came up with the following as I began to accept the new reality: *Sometimes bad things happen to good people, and it doesn't all work out. Period. I can work toward good outcomes, but I will radically accept life as it is and seek the freedom that comes with that.*

The next new rule that came out of my "funeral" for this belief was this: *life can be good and beautiful, even in the wake of terrible events.* Even saddled right next to terrible things, I have the ability to appreciate life.

Bad things still happen, and it doesn't all work out; my job is to let go of things I can't control and move into acceptance rather than insisting that because I'm a good person, only good things should happen.

Old Belief—If I Do Good, I Will Receive Good

New rule: *do as much good as I can in this life.* This new approach alleviates my former expectation of reciprocity. I no longer feel entitled to goodness from God and others, and instead focus on an overarching value that matters to me, doing good in this life. When I let my core values guide my purpose and my actions, rather than an outdated belief, it helps me find freedom and let go of the need for a particular outcome. This more mature approach allows me to let go of negative or difficult situations, tantrums, and controlling behavior and clears space for me to do more. It better serves me and those around me.

Old Belief—Others Should Believe and Act the Way I Do

This one is a sneaky core belief that most people have running in the back of their minds, like an operating system on a computer. When certain programs are running in the background on your computer—JavaScript, Microsoft Windows, or macOS—these operating systems are rather quiet but strong (just like our core beliefs). The quickest way to know if you have this limiting core belief is to get in the presence of somebody who behaves and believes differently than you. The limiting belief will surface with a vengeance. For instance, the Black Lives Matter movement, the COVID-19 pandemic, and the American politics of 2020 brought to the forefront the tremendous division that exists in America based on beliefs about race, finances, healthcare, and politics.

To update this belief, I created a new core operating program for myself: *People make choices that I can't control and that I might not like. I can choose to release my expectation that others should live by my values and beliefs and learn to love them as they are, not as I think they should be.* This helps me to reduce my urge to control and criticize others who are not doing life the way I believe they should. And neither am I at the mercy of people who are different from me, even the ones in my own family.

Below is a list of other beliefs to which I have said goodbye and the new beliefs I created in their place.

I must say goodbye to my beliefs that...

- life is mostly safe;

- God will work all things together for the good in *this* life;

- if I pray hard enough and have strong enough faith, I can change the things I don't like; and

- that clean living = a positive, happy life.

I must begin to accept that...

- I can do my best to make myself and my family safe through education, personal responsibility, and wise choices, but ultimately, I cannot foolproof life;

- God is more interested in my character than my comfort (thanks, Rick Warren);

- God is not a vending machine where I put in my good behaviors (prayers, tithes, clean living), and he delivers the outcomes I'm looking for; instead, I do everything I can in a challenging situation to find a remedy and make things right, I reach out to Him to steady me through life's difficulties and draw on the strength of His presence, but life's outcomes are often out of my hands; and

- I will do my best to be healthy and happy, but life is not always fair.

Kendra: Updating the Rule Book

Returning to the example I shared in Chapter 1 of my client Kendra whose older brother died when she was eight years old, Kendra had long-standing beliefs about abandonment and rejection. Because of her brother's death and the way her family managed it, Kendra believed—deep in her internal operating system—that warm, trusting relationships were scarce, and that people she loved would eventually leave. She dealt with this by locking down her emotions, disconnecting from others, and getting busy being successful and perfect. When I met her, she had an overdeveloped career and financial life, was distant from her own children, had loads of self-hatred, and walked around with an underdeveloped ability to show up as a healthy adult in relationships. In short, she had a lot of money but was lonely and unfulfilled.

To move forward, she had to update her rule book. It might look something like this:

I must say goodbye to the beliefs that...

- I will be abandoned, and life is unstable all the time; because I believe this, I either over-disclose in relationships with the wrong people, or I avoid good, solid partner options because of my fears;

- success and perfection lead to happiness;

- keeping my deeper emotions hidden is best for me; and

- that controlling others makes me feel better than allowing them to be who they are, I feel afraid if I cannot make them do what I think they should, and I feel safe when I tell other people how they should behave.

I must begin to believe and accept that...

- most people in my life have not actually left me; my nervous system is extra-sensitive because of my loss, but I am surrounded by several caring people;

- when I investigate my reality (and not just my thoughts or feelings), I see that life is more stable than my feelings tell me it is; I can slow myself down to get to know others rather than attaching too quickly and then moving away from them when they won't let me control them;

- success does feel good, but it's not guaranteed to bring happiness; I can investigate other sources of researched and verifiable ways to experience happiness;

- when I express my deepest emotions in a safe setting, I help myself and feel better; I also experience safe intimacy with others which feels so good;

- I am a steward, not a warden, for my children; healthy parenting practices allow me to guide and shepherd them using love and logic rather than just grades, performance, and gold stars, which can leave us both empty in the end; and

- I can focus on progress, not perfection.

* * *

Now, do this exercise for yourself. Can you identify a previously hidden belief you had about yourself or the world and then create a new one that offers you more freedom and space?

I must say goodbye to my belief that...

_____

_____

_____

I must begin to accept that...

_____

_____

_____

FORMULATING THE ESSENCE
OF THE LESSON

You may be reading this and thinking *what if I don't know the lesson; is there anything I can do to mine that out?* If so, my suggestion is that you observe what you talk about when you share about your loss and look for ways you can honestly expand your sights. For example, after a traumatic event such as the unexpected death of a loved one, a partner's affair, or an abrupt layoff from work, a natural response to such jolting news would be to believe that *life is not fair*. When life blindsides us, indeed we feel victimized and vulnerable; our innocence is lost. However, that same response months or years later, if left unchecked, could greatly undermine our well-being. If you remain stuck in a polluted belief system about yourself and about life, it can greatly hamper your health. You may be hard to live with and risk alienating yourself from crucial opportunities that lie ahead. In time, it's essential to learn how to reframe the situation, at least a little. You can begin the work of reframing the story of your life by adding one little word to your narrative: *and.*

The Essential *And*

When we enter into our own stories as narrators rather than just characters at the whim of someone else's storyline, we can take the driver's seat of our own lives and begin to feel empowered. Here's how: when we reflect on what caused us to be broken open, inserting the word "and" somewhere in the narrative can help us grow.

At thirty-one, I was pregnant, and I was diagnosed with cancer. It was the worst thing that had ever happened to me, *and* that entire ordeal eventually shaped my career choices, led me back to school, helped me develop a compass for handling future tough things, and led me to write this book. It was the story itself that set the stage for growth. In the wake of my suffering, I found that my belief systems were inadequate to support me through my difficulties. I needed to find a new way to think and a way to find my footing in the rushing river of my reality. Life "schooled" me when adversity revealed that my "beginner beliefs" couldn't keep me afloat when my lifeboat capsized and I couldn't find a life jacket.

It was in the "and" that I found my footing and a springboard for the rest of my life. Through a hectic and messy process involving disappointments, physical suffering, emotional upheaval, disbelief, coming undone, and falling down, I was able to rewrite my story. The work of healing from a life-threatening illness while raising a family crushed by catastrophe was daunting. But eventually, it helped me define my most essential values, invigorate my immature faith, and solidify my identity in something other than my appearance, my youth, my education, and my health. All of this happened in the "and" of that story. I now refer to this work of crunching through our losses to find what's left and do what's next, the Essential *And.*

* * *

Here are some more examples. They may not be everyone's experience or beliefs, but see if you can find pieces of your own experience within these stories.

Miscarriage and Infertility

Many women who cannot conceive or carry a baby to term may be understandably plagued by guilt, shame, and anger. Feeling adrift, a woman may feel like life is a rip-off. A woman carrying this belief about life is at risk of creating intense personal torment for herself and others. No one would argue that a woman who'd experienced multiple miscarriages and infertility wouldn't have a deep sadness her entire life based on being deprived of motherhood. But years later, their partners may grow tired of supporting their relentless sadness; friends and loved ones end up walking on eggshells or avoid announcing their own pregnancy news. Everyone, including the person who's stuck, is picking up the tab on this unmanaged and unprocessed grief response.

Old beliefs might include the following:

- I am incomplete.

- Life is unfair.

- No one understands.

- Life should be different than it is.

Essential And statement

Instead, she could try a version of the following statements:

- I feel incomplete as a woman, *and* I am working on radically accepting what is. I don't like it, but I notice that when I'm defiant about what I should be getting, I get even less of what I want from others around me and from myself.

- I wish life was different, *and* I am finding a part of life I never knew existed, through intimate friendships with others who could not have children either. I feel alive in their presence and like I am truly seen and heard. They understand me.

- It still pains me when I see moms and their babies or hear about another one of my friends who is expecting, *and* I am learning to nurture and affirm the presence of an unmet longing within myself rather than taking it out on those I love.

Loss of a Child to Suicide

Any parent who has endured the unimaginable pain of losing a child will tell you there is no worse torment. As one parent told me, this thorny path deems grief-stricken parents "part of a club no one wants to be in, and you can never get out of."

On the list of life's greatest stressors and most difficult of storylines, this one is at the top. Even worse, for a parent of a child who died by suicide, there is gut-wrenching shame and self-reproach that can only be compared to the feeling of being immersed in a vat of emotional battery acid. The wicked questioning, self-doubt, replaying of every conversation, and searching for clues that could've prevented their death is only half the problem. For some, there's a guilty relief knowing their child is no longer suffering and is now at peace. They wonder: *should a parent ever be glad their own child is dead?* Their child seemed to be in constant crisis, and the parent on the other side felt powerless to help them, yet constantly held hostage by their threats. Not only are these parents simultaneously longing for their child, heartbroken by their child's decision to end their life, but they must also face the scrutiny of everyone around them. The other torrid reality a parent-survivor must face is learning to walk through life while everyone is (secretly, and not so secretly) wondering what kind of parent they were.

Some parents may mistakenly believe that they had the power to make their child want to live, and if they could just have given enough care, love, encouragement, doctors, diagnoses, and counseling, then life never would've gone this way. If they are unable to move out of this "fallacy of control" belief system, they may be tormented for the rest of their lives. Learning new skills and tools for enduring, releasing, and accepting the choices of others, and their own powerlessness over others, will set them free. I've seen parents so immobilized by their fear and disbelief that they've lost sight of the family members who still remain. They've become a shadow of their former selves, longing for what they cannot have and often missing what's still left.

Essential And Statement

*After doing everything to try and help her, our daughter, who suffered from depression and despair, took her own life. I will never totally understand why. My heart and life have shattered into a million pieces. I miss her every day, **and** the strength I've found in my faith (or in the rest of my family or friends) is unlike anything I ever imagined. I feel carried, helped, and reassured, and I hope that my daughter and I will be together again. I never knew a spiritual love like this existed until I went through this horrible nightmare. I would never wish this for another parent, but I've also tapped into strength and endurance I didn't realize I had. Other parents have been reaching* *out to me for help, and I feel so purposeful in my life—like never before. I've gotten out of bed the last three days. Tomorrow, maybe not. And that's OK.*

Divorce

Finally, a wife who explains the devastation of divorce after being married for twenty-seven years and how she's just beginning to thread her Essential *And* work around the edges of her experience:

My husband told me he doesn't love me and hasn't for quite some time. Not only has he filed for divorce but he's already on dating sites. I have been so bitter. After all I did for him! The thing is though, I finally realized that I did so much for him and our kids, that I didn't ever take care of myself. Somehow, I thought my kids and husband would do for me what I had done for them all along. I was furious at all of them. I totally gave myself away to take care of them and then there was nothing left for me. My kids grew up, got married, and went off to school. They left me! And then my husband left, too. The nerve. I did everything for him. He's so selfish. When I looked in the mirror the day after the divorce was final, I was spitting nails, first at him, but then at myself. I had lost myself over the last three decades, and now, finally, I'm trying to find myself again. Maybe for the first time. I did not give permission for this to happen, **and** *I am learning how to look at myself in a new light and begin to take care of myself.*

A person who stays stuck in their old belief systems about the loss of their marriage is at risk of carrying their "poor me" and "he was the Big Bad Wolf" beliefs right into their next relationship. It's no wonder second and third marriages have a greater than 70 percent failure rate. Unless the two new partners do some pretty heavy lifting on what happened the first time around—examine what their part was and take responsibility for it, make the necessary changes within themselves, and update their individual operating systems—the relationship is doomed to fail. Even worse, they're doomed to pass that same operating system on to their children. One woman I know actually said, "Forgive him? Are you kidding me? My bitterness and anger toward him are the energy I use to get through my everyday life!" That's quite a legacy to hand over to her kids, don't you think?

* * *

Can you see that someone who's undergone real tragedy and is now leaning into the transformative power of the change process must be sure their beliefs keep pace with their new life? The butterfly no longer crawls on the ground like a caterpillar, neither should its beliefs.

---

*Note: doing the work of the Essential **And** in your own life may feel like you're being stretched, uncomfortable, or in pain. But this is what growth feels like. Keep going! I can see your wings beginning to shine through your chrysalis as you hang adrift through the dark night, uncertain of what the morning will bring. It's happening; you're on your way.*

Once you understand how life *really* is, things will be easier for you. Well, no, that's not true; it won't be easier. A good life is not an *easy* life. Courageous people are not developed by having good and easy lives. The people I like to spend time with, the ones who can lead and who tend to make a difference, are the ones who are soul-deep, bomb-proof, and pretty gritty from all the brush-ups they've been in. And they didn't get there by having easy lives. By doing this work now, we can start to see some of the takeaways from our experiences and empower ourselves with the present moment. In the next chapter, we'll continue to build a framework within ourselves for moving through loss.

Chapter 6

Lessons Learned
from Living

"What is to give light, must endure burning."

—VIKTOR FRANKL

CREATING MEANING FROM LOSS

A young physician in 1940s Austria was faced with a life-changing decision. Newly married and ready to leverage his career by going to America to expand his practice, the acclaimed psychiatrist and neurologist was confronted with a harrowing choice: either accept the invitation to America and escape the impending Nazi torture that had ripped through his Homeland, or stay the course and stand beside his parents in a concentration camp.

Upon seeking spiritual guidance in this vexing decision, he decided to follow a sign given to him, which was to honor his father and mother. He decided to become imprisoned alongside them and his wife. For three years, he and his family descended into hell in the Auschwitz and Dachau concentration camps. After miraculously surviving, but also enduring the death of his wife, both of his parents, and hundreds of his peers, Dr. Frankl emerged a Holocaust survivor. He sat down, traumatized but inspired, and wrote his now famous and oft-quoted bestselling book *Man's Search for Meaning*. He completed the book in just nine days. Here's an excerpt:

> *Even though conditions such as lack of sleep, insufficient food and various mental stresses may suggest that the inmates were bound to react in certain ways, in the final analysis, it becomes clear that the sort of person the prisoner became was the result of an inner decision and not the result of the camp influences alone. Fundamentally, then, any man can, under such circumstances decide what shall become of him—mentally and spiritually.*

In his book, Frankl lists five profound lessons that he took from his experience:

1. We always retain the ability to choose our attitude.

2. There will be suffering. It's how we react to suffering that counts.

3. The power of purpose.

4. The test of our true character is revealed in how we act.

5. Human kindness can be found in the most surprising places.

His bestselling book has now sold more than ten million copies. His work is sought after, and he has comforted and guided even millions more as they followed his readings and teachings. In his courage to face adversity, he saved numerous of his fellow men from the clutches of their Punisher, and still hundreds more were the recipient of his comfort in ministry, in the dregs of the camps amid the torture and madness.

Although Dr. Frankl lost what seems like his entire life, what he found were lessons that transformed not only his life but the lives of people throughout time and eternity.

EACH EXPERIENCE IS YOUR TEACHER

Lessons Learned from Living is where we gather the nuggets of what your loss has taught you. It could be about a range of different aspects, such as

- how the loved one went through life;

- what you learned from that person (both positive and negative);

- takeaways from their life; or

- things you witnessed or watched along the dark path you've been walking.

Many of us are not aware that the person or thing we lost and the associated grief is speaking to us. Grief is trying to deliver multiple messages: information, inspiration, or if we're lucky, transformation. From our process of knowing them or of losing them, we can glean some alchemy for ourselves. This person's life instructs and leads us either as a cautionary tale, or by helping us formulate next steps.

If you came to this book searching to make sense of the loss, you may not realize that purpose is being spoken to you through the things you are avoiding the most.

It's possible you may not yet feel ready for this chapter. If you picked up the book and have made it this far, chances are, you may be feeling ready for the catalyst. If you're just home from the funeral or just out of divorce court—if you're too close to your grief and it still feels fresh—I invite you to spend additional time in Chapters 2 through 5 to process your grief fully. Or put this book down and come back to it when you feel ready. Or maybe you are ready now. Everyone processes grief differently. Lessons come into focus and get delivered to us at different times.

EXERCISE—LESSONS LEARNED FROM LIVING

The idea now is to get into action around your loss. It's time to take your grief and do something with it. List specific action steps you can take to create some clarity around your loss.

Step 1: Who or what did you lose?

The goal of working through this particular question is to determine the nature of your loss. It may be the loss of a person, a job, a pet, or a divorce, for example.

Step 2: Sift through this event, person, or relationship for meaning.

What can you note about it? What stands out to you? What do you remember most about it or about them? If there was a highlight reel of the event or a series of low points in the relationship, what were they?

Step 3: What is the lesson learned?

If you were able to sift through all the highlights and lowlights of that person's life, write down the bottom-line takeaways from their life.

What did you observe or witness about them? What did you love about them? What ways of being or actions would you like to emulate? What do you want to make a point of doing in your own life or not doing in your own life?

Step 4: Today, I will...

Take the information in Step 3 and write down an actionable item or step for yourself.

An example of this would be a tenderhearted mother of four daughters I know who lost her mother from late-diagnosed uterine cancer. Her mom was such a giver to her whole family but didn't take proper care of herself. This meant she had avoided the signs her body was giving her, and by the time doctors found the cancer, she only had a few months to live. Now her daughter, in the wake of losing her mom, began experiencing pain and discomfort in her pelvis. Her mother's life and death became like a 911 call for her to attend to her own health. The lesson: her mother's life beckoned her to take care of her own.

Are there actionable steps for you to take in life as a direct result of your loss?

LESSONS LEARNED FROM COLIN— A PERSONAL EXAMPLE

Continuing with my personal example from Chapter 4, here are some examples of lessons I learned with the loss of our son's friend Colin, who we considered a family member. This is distinct from the Lost and Found activity of Chapter 4, where you have physically lost someone or something, but it can be an extension of that activity. For me, what still remained was his sister and my son's other friends that were bright spots in my life. Realizing this was a big headline for me: *wow, I had no idea until this person died that these truths were viable or evident.*

Lesson 1

Life can be very short.

Colin died when he was eighteen. And this helped me to

crystallize the idea that tomorrow is not guaranteed. None of us know when our time is up, and we should appreciate the beauty and value of what we have right here in the moment. We could apply the same lesson to losing a job, going through a divorce, or losing a pet; the instant we lose something, it becomes crystal clear what we had and its value to us.

Lesson 2

Pay attention to the now.

This was an invitation for me to be more mindful, to treasure people rather than things, and perhaps to not prioritize stuff that doesn't have eternal value.

Lesson 3

Give people space after they have experienced a tragic loss.

A few hours after we found out that Colin had died, we called his parents at 4:00 in the morning. What a terrible call for them to receive! By 9:00 a.m. or 10:00 a.m., his sister, aunt, and uncle came to our house and removed all of his belongings. My husband, my son, and I sat on the couch. The towel he had used to dry himself after his shower the night before was still wet on the towel rack. Within half an hour, every glimpse of Colin's presence in our home was removed.

Colin's family was trying to hold on to any piece of him they could find. They were traumatized, and it makes 100 percent sense to me why they did that. It was a grief response. In retrospect, it was jolting for my son, husband, and me and added an additional layer of shock and trauma to our loss. This is not to take away from their loss or say they shouldn't have taken these actions; I am sharing our grief and our lessons learned from the loss we experienced. In their position, I probably would've done the same thing just to try to hold one more thing of his to smell his scent.

Sometimes people need to move slowly and not experience too many changes too soon after a big loss. Grief literature consistently recommends not making a big decision for a year after a traumatic loss. Drastic, unexpected changes upend your life. Giving people space after they have a loss allows them to regain their footing and move through their new reality at their own pace. Moving forward, I would be able to react with more empathy and awareness, not only for myself and my family but for my clients and my friends who go through loss.

Lesson 4

Celebrate and be in the moment with loved ones.

I've said this throughout the book, but it bears repeating. Once people or the job or the pet is gone, we lose the ability to savor and enjoy the present moment with them. Once time runs out, it doesn't ever run back in. It's not like when the tide goes out. Once it's done, it's done.

Celebrating the people you love with intention is a practice in our very busy, efficient, multitasking culture that many of us do not do. We will live with the assumption that if I saw this person this morning, I will see them again tonight. If I told them I loved them yesterday, there's no need to do it today. The lesson learned, for me, is to celebrate those you love and make sure they know how you feel.

Today, I Will...

This is the next part of the lesson, using my experience with Colin's death as the example.

I will take them however I get them. Colin filled the space left when my eldest son went to college. I didn't choose to have him move here. I didn't expect that kid in my life. None of us did. It just unfolded in that way. I didn't realize at the time what a special young man he was. I have since determined that if people are placed in my life and we begin to develop a special relationship, I'm going to allow that and not have specific barriers or definitions around the friendship or relationship. I'm going to see the people that life brings to me as opportunities for rich connection and more easily accept people into my life.

Never miss a hug. I appreciate physical contact and the special feeling of someone in my arms. Since doing this activity for the first time, I've elevated the importance of all hugs from loved ones. Now, upon greeting or parting from someone I love, when we embrace, I take a picture in my mind, as if this were the last time that I would get to hold them. To myself, I whisper a hope that they fully know the sensation and the security of the love that we share. I savor it and try to stay in it a few extra beats if they'll let me. I get to experience the exchange of love between us as if there is a golden cord or a living, pulsing live wire, a highway where the love is palpable. It's rare to be in someone's presence and feel how much they love us. That sensation can't be found anywhere else. So today, I never miss an opportunity for that exchange with my people, even if only for a few moments.

Now, answer these questions for yourself:

- Who was your relationship with?

- What was the lesson learned?

- Today, I will...

The way you tell the story about the loss provides clues to the lessons you're meant to learn. Those nuggets are the highlight reel of how you're processing this loss—how you make sense of it, what you think about it, and how you spin it to yourself and others. Those thoughts, beliefs, and views should lead you to questions such as *Is this a lesson for me? Is this true? Is this helpful to think about it this way?* I often describe it as an investigation of your beliefs about what happened. And they are all clues, so you might not want to do this exercise before understanding what you believe about life. If you're uncertain, return to Chapter 4 before proceeding.

IT'S NOT THE LOSS; IT'S FACING THE LOSS

The reason I know that loss can be a catalyst and provoke growth is because there are people who don't go through significant loss, disruption, or trauma. And when they don't have those experiences, they go looking for them. As I shared in Chapter 4, pain has a purpose. There is an inherent wonder in overcoming hard things, learning about ourselves, and being pushed to our limits.

For instance, mountain climbing is difficult for the average person. The gear, the tremendous physical effort, being under exertion at altitude, coping with extreme weather conditions, the risk of wildlife, the technical skills needed—it's a lot to handle. But to hear those who summit dangerous peaks, you'd think they had won the life lottery by the glow on their faces. Their satisfaction and sense of accomplishment has come to them hard-won after enduring high winds and dust on a narrow trail, getting lost and then reoriented in a snowstorm, climbing back down a steep, icy trail, or facing a mountain lion with little to protect them other than some climbing poles and banging on a tin can. They are ecstatic. Over the moon. Why? They set out to face a challenge, to push themselves beyond their limits, to stretch beyond themselves, and take on a huge challenge. In searching for the struggle, they discovered the gold within that experience. They found a new sense of self when they signed on for the risk, danger, and unknown challenges of the mountain. Human identity and well-being are cosmically wrapped up in overcoming challenges. It's as if the facing of these feats of physical endurance is what makes us. *It's not the loss; it's facing the loss.* It strengthens the endurance muscle inside of us, which in turn allows us to feel self-confidence and empowerment.

When you look at loss as the doorway to genuinely helping you become who you are meant to be, the energy around you will change. It can't necessarily be right at the moment of the loss; you're not thinking about how you can grow and develop it because you're mostly just shattered. But when the time is right, taking your individual losses, disappointments, traumas, and core-shaking events and beginning the brave process of mining them to their depths is what you came to this book for. On the other side of this loss, satisfaction, centeredness, and confidence awaits; developing a high capacity to manage and do difficult things and help others will lead to feeling masterful.

WOUND DEBRIDEMENT

Not taking the time now to sort through your losses will make it harder for your heartbreak to heal. If you can't jump into the stream, move with the losses, get in the flow, and try to understand the lessons from your toil, you'll remain stuck, similar to an injury in the body. When wounds or incisions in the body close without being thoroughly cleaned, they can get infected, and things can get worse.

I used to work in a hospital, and when an injured patient comes in with a wound, the hospital staff has to clean it out before they can medicate and pack it with dressing so it can heal. This is the process of wound debridement. Sometimes the cleaning of a wound is so painful for the patient that they're sedated so they can tolerate it. If you close that wound before it's properly cleaned, before all foreign matters like dirt and debris are removed, an infection is almost guaranteed. To ensure proper healing and restoration of body and health, and to prevent future problems, that painful process of wound debridement is absolutely essential. In fact, hospital staff would be considered careless and negligent if they didn't perform it on an open wound. Painful but necessary. So too is your work around these losses.

When life deals us a blow and we are traumatized through loss, if we try to close that wound and move on, what ends up happening are parallels of infections in our life. If what we have been through—the loss, the depression, the anger—doesn't have anywhere to go, it usually goes inside. And if we don't give it room, a voice, and a way to release, then it can come out sideways. When you push your feelings down, eventually they'll come out in ways you don't want: severe depression, inability to get out of bed, addiction, anger problems, overspending, gambling, living contrary to your values—any way to try and quiet all the shadows left inside. That wound is underneath, festering and infected.

BECOMING WHO YOU WERE ALWAYS MEANT TO BE

John Piper, a leader in Minneapolis going through cancer, gave a presentation. He later published it as a pamphlet entitled *Don't Waste Your Cancer*. The idea in his presentation was that the entire journey of what he referred to as "the dark night of your soul" is an invitation to go somewhere else and grow as a person, to allow yourself to be broken down so that you can rebuild and reinvent yourself. Viktor Frankl came to the same conclusion: suffering is a doorway and all loss is a doorway to your next steps in life.

In the next chapter, we will focus on finding your voice.

Chapter 7

The Dear Letters

"The only way out is through."

—ROBERT FROST

"Write what disturbs you, what you fear, what you have not been willing to speak about. Be willing to be split open."

—NATALIE GOLDBERG

Newlyweds Heather and Joel celebrated finding each other. In their mid-twenties, they were thrilled to have found "the one" and happily pledged their lives together in marriage. Even more thrilling, the next year, Heather discovered she was pregnant. What a dream come true! Joel, a young survivor of cancer, had wondered if he'd even be able to father children after going through cancer treatments, which can rob many survivors of their fertility. What a miracle! They were going to be parents.

At their initial checkup, seeing the baby for the first time should've been a thrill. But at two months pregnant, the thrill turned to shock when they learned not only that Heather was carrying twins but also that neither baby had a heartbeat. Joel and Heather wept.

Months later, Heather became pregnant again. They were all at once elated and terrified for their new baby's safety. When the first trimester passed, they celebrated and held each other close; this time, their baby had made it out of the danger zone of early pregnancy. She was safe! It finally felt like a reality, and they allowed themselves the hope of bringing their baby girl home. They named her Skylar and counted down the days until they could finally hold their daughter.

In mid-December, at full term, Heather noticed Skylar wasn't moving as much. She told Joel, and they frantically made their way to the hospital. Doctors confirmed their worst fears—Skylar was a healthy weight and had gone full term, but she had also died. After hours of labor, Heather and Joel sat devastated near the little life they had thought they'd get to take home. Skylar Grace never got to meet her parents face to face.

A year later, Heather and Joel finally got to bring a baby home, little Eliana (whose name means "God has answered"). But the excitement and rush of becoming parents was tinged with pain as they remembered their losses. Heather attended a support group, led by other parents, to manage the grief of losing her other children. She also wrote letters to both Joel and Eliana as a way to make sense of the losses. In her moving letter to Joel on their anniversary, she wrote this:

Today, as we watched our wedding video...I couldn't help but look back at four-years-younger us and think about how little I knew back then. How little I knew about my very real weaknesses, about the trials we'd face, the losses we'd share, and the tense moments we'd wade through. I also couldn't have imagined the growth we'd experience. The family we'd fight for, and the joy and peace I'd have, knowing the depth of strength and safety found in the hand I'd hold through it all. It's been an unforgettable four years, to say the least, but today, I can't say enough how thankful I am to be your wife. It is truly an honor. I love you, Joel Clark. Happy anniversary.

And to her first daughter Skylar, on the second anniversary of her death, she wrote this:

I can't believe it would have been your second birthday today, my sweet Skylar Grace. My firstborn daughter. I miss you so much.

This year has been the definition of bittersweet as it's held so much joy when we added your little sister to our family, and yet watching her grow reminds me of what we missed experiencing with you. All the dreams we had for your life. All the personality quirks I never got to know. Eyes I didn't get to see. Laughs I never heard. I'm still confused and wonder why. And a little bitter that this is our story. But I know there are lessons you've taught us that no one else can. Friendships that have been formed and lives impacted because of your life. And you have made me a better mom. I'm sure of it. I love you, sweet girl. Miss you always.

—Mom

WHY SHOULD I WRITE
A DEAR LETTER?

The Dear Letter tool helps you put your experience into words and digest your loss, enabling you to move through it and ultimately move on. Often, many who face the despair of losing someone or something they valued feel disempowered, lacking control over their situation. The Dear Letters are an opportunity to find your voice, regain your footing, and reclaim some agency over your life.

Not long ago, I read an article from a lawyer that talked about how attorneys are taught to persuade jurors during trial. One of the points of the article is that people hire attorneys for many different reasons. Obviously, people hire attorneys for different types of cases and to represent them in criminal and civil matters. But something I didn't know was that people sometimes hire attorneys even though they know they probably won't win their case, just so they can hear somebody argue their side of the matter. Hearing an advocate step up on their behalf is very satisfying for somebody going through a dispute, lawsuit, or court case. Having a representative talk about what happened, their feelings, their beliefs, the evidence, and the rationale—essentially their point of view in the entire matter—can be incredibly cathartic.

Writing a Dear Letter espouses this same idea: this is the opportunity to speak what is true for you and give voice to what has been left unsaid around your grief. All the things you wish you could've said or should've said can find their place and finally be outed. Especially the gritty stuff.

Unloading your thoughts and putting words on paper creates a clearing to see what is beneath. Often, new information begins to emerge.

The most important thing to know is that these letters don't need to be sent. In fact, sending them can disrupt the act of processing your story, loss, or grief. As soon as you start to write a letter to an actual person, that you'd stamp and mail, it changes the nature and purpose of the letter. Now you have an audience. You start to have a dialogue in your mind about what you're saying. And then you will inherently start editing yourself based on your opinion about what you think the other person is going to think. Rather than writing the version you're going to mail, I'd like you to write unedited, with nobody looking over your shoulder. Say what you need to say and what you're not sure you want anybody else to read. This exercise is for you, not for anybody else.

REPAIRING RELATIONSHIP
WITH SELF AND OTHERS

I offer multiple categories and writing prompts in this chapter. As you look through them, my hope is that one or more of these phrases will spark some thought for you. Magic can happen during the process of writing your thoughts on the page. Where previously these words have been rattling around in your head, they now have a place to go. And if you don't have words or phrases yet, that's OK; I'll bet at least you have feelings because your loss has been left unexpressed inside of you. It could be a heavy emotion, a sense of regret, or a sinking feeling. Writing it down can begin to ravel it back up, like winding strands of yarn back onto a spool. Just write what you're experiencing: heaviness in your head, a crushing feeling on your shoulders, stomachaches, headaches that keep coming back. *Write it down.*

Once you give it a little nudge, the words about your experiences themselves become like ushers in a theater, showing you to your seat. First, you might notice a stomachache. You write that down, and once acknowledged, the cramps in your gut suddenly become your guide, and then you tune in to what else is happening. Perhaps you're sitting in a clenched ball, trying to brace yourself against the pain. This might be causing shoulder pain, headaches, or other physical responses to grief, like a stomachache. Write that down, and give yourself permission to be kind to yourself and take a warm bath, place your hand on your heart, and even relax a little as you move through your day, going easy on yourself as you realize your entire being is impacted by this loss. Writing down words about what you are experiencing (*I have a stomachache*) ushers you right to the seat you need to be in—permission to be kind to yourself.

Let me share an example. Let's say you went through a very difficult time—a lawsuit, loss of your business, or a catastrophic illness—and you had certain friends that didn't check up on you, were not around, or didn't offer to help, and you're feeling incomplete and quite sad or mad about it. It makes sense to feel that way. Rather than drawing closer as you had hoped, it may seem that instead, your friends disappeared. And now, there's a pebble in your shoe, so to speak—or something bigger, like a thorn in your side—about why they weren't there. That Dear Letter is one I like to call "Missing in Action." Writing a Dear Letter will allow you to get clear about the specific upset within the collateral loss. You may feel slighted because they haven't checked up on you. You may feel that they aren't reciprocating your contribution and support to them. You may be questioning the depth of your friendship; perhaps you thought you were closer. You may feel an offense begin to rise whenever you think about that person. Write that down.

Often when we go through something hard, we feel it's meant to be carried by the community of people around us.

Community is a protective factor discussed in Chapter 4; we support each other, we celebrate joyous events, and we grieve together. When part of our community doesn't show up, the mind begins to fill in the blanks in a corrosive way. We may get lost in a maze of negative thoughts about other people, and deep wounds emerge within us that can derail our future happiness. Rather than work through these offenses, people sometimes choose to totally cut these friends out of their lives. Lacking other gears for handling such hurt, they downshift into "cut off" mode rather than "let's talk about it" mode. As they go through life, rather than grow richer from deep relationships they've built through good times and bad, they become bitter and blameful as they hold on to long lists of everything others have done to them.

Seeing Through Multiple Lenses

We see other people in our lives through *our own lens* of background and experiences. No one else has the exact same lens as you do. Even within the same family, they don't have the same background, the same upbringing, or the same experiences. One sibling can have a very different experience of a parent than their brother or sister does. When we can't understand how a person could act in a particular situation, it's because that's not something *we* would do based on our own past, family upbringing, or the myriad of other factors that make up who we are. Looking at a situation from another person's point of view and realizing something as profound and simple as *they were never shown how to do things the way I was* could be incredibly powerful.

When people act in ways that surprise or confuse me, it is now my privilege to look at them with curiosity and ask *why would they do that?* Here's an even bigger question: *how come they don't do that more often, given all the things that have happened to them?* The fact that it only happened once is surprising, given where they come from, who they are, and what they've been through.

You may lose a good friendship over a traumatic event; however, with a little care, understanding, and processing, you may be able to retain that valued friendship. A family I know recently went through the difficulty of having their adult daughter live away from home in a therapeutic setting for a year and a half. The family had some deep internal problems, and the daughter's struggles could only be managed if she lived somewhere else, where she could get the support she needed. While their daughter was away, some particularly good friends lost touch with them and failed to check up on them for the first nine months. The husband and wife were taken aback, offended that their old friends had not known what was going on in their lives because they hadn't called or heard through the grapevine. When they did more checking, they found out that these friends had gone through the loss of a family member and didn't have the extra bandwidth to reach out and care for anybody outside their immediate borders. This simple piece of information completely shifted the dynamics of the friendship. Suddenly, doors were open, and once they both had an understanding of the other's situation, they rekindled their friendship. That's a simple, straightforward example, but sometimes we don't get missing information that restores the friendship, so you have to do the work yourself.

THE DEAR LETTER PROMPTS

DEAR LETTERS
WHEN I GO THROUGH A DIVORCE

☐ Dear Ex ☐ Dear Judge ☐ Dear Married Friends

☐ Dear Kids ☐ Dear Family ☐ To the betrayal partner

DEAR LETTERS
CATASTROPHIC ILLNESS

☐ Dear Illness ☐ Dear Healthy People ☐ Dear My Body

☐ Dear God ☐ Dear Family

WHEN GRIEF IS GOOD

WHEN MY LOVED ONE DIED SUDDENLY

- ☐ Dear God
- ☐ Dear Loved One
- ☐ Dear Onlookers or First Responders
- ☐ Dear Death

LETTER TO A FRIEND WHO WASN'T THERE DURING MY LOSS

- ☐ Dear "Missing in Action"
- ☐ Dear all the people who *were* there

WHEN MY LOVED ONE DIED BY SUICIDE OR OVERDOSE

- ☐ Dear Loved One
- ☐ Dear Suicide
- ☐ Dear Darkness
- ☐ Dear Addiction
- ☐ Dear Overdose Drug
- ☐ Dear Other Parents

WHEN MY LOVED ONE DIED BY VIOLENCE

- ☐ To the Perpetrator
- ☐ To the Police officer
- ☐ To the Legal System

WHEN MY CHILD DIED

- ☐ Dear God
- ☐ Dear Other Parents
- ☐ Dear Child
- ☐ Dear Family

DEAR LETTERS
WHEN I AM ANGRY WITH THE ONE I LOST

☐ Dear Loved One

DEAR LETTERS
WHEN MY LOVED ONE DIED
FROM AN ILLNESS

☐ Dear Cancer   ☐ Dear Healthcare   ☐ Dear Helpers
                          System or Doctors
☐ Dear Disease

DEAR LETTERS
WHEN I AM ANGRY AT SPECIFIC
PEOPLE AFTER A LOVED ONE DIES

☐ Dear Family   ☐ Dear Church

☐ Dear Friends   ☐ Dear Healthcare System

DEAR LETTERS
WHEN I LOST SOMEONE I LOVED
AFTER PROLONGED CARETAKING

☐ Dear Life   ☐ Dear Normal People   ☐ Dear Loved One

Step 1

Write out what you have lost. A list of collateral losses was listed in Chapter 4. Please refer to that list if you need a refresher:

- What I lost, miss, wish I had, feel like, or notice is...

- The expectations I held and why I feel disappointed

- How I feel about that person not being there

This can help you get your hands around what is happening.

Another way of writing this is by using the following prompts:

- I feel...

- I fear...

- I had hoped for...

- I expected...

This can help shine a light on your hurt, your judgments, and what you wish would've happened. By laying this out, you can begin to lessen its hold on you and move away from bitterness, heavy emotions, and limiting beliefs.

Dear _____,

_____

_____

_____

Signed, _____

Once you write down your feelings, your fear, and your unmet hopes and expectations, you can begin to take your next steps and decide whether you want to reach out to this person in real time. If so, you certainly don't want to reach out when you feel angry and disappointed.

Step 2

If you hope to heal the relationship, the next step is to get clarity and begin to formulate your goals. If you discover your goal is to maintain or restore that friendship, you can then decide how you want to show up in your contact with them.

On the other hand, if your goal is to express your anger and frustration and feel heard—like your own attorney at a hearing—then write about that. A lot of times, you discover you are misplacing the anger components of your grief and projecting them onto another person. That is important information. While it's true that you *did* have this loss, and they *weren't* there the way you had hoped, it's also true that it's not their responsibility to be the container for your anger. You may have some unjustified anger that's misdirected at an old friend. Rather than opening a torrent of upset on them, maybe you need to step back and do for yourself what you wish they would've done for you.

In her novel *Crooked Little Heart*, Anne Lamott writes: "Expectations are just resentments waiting to happen." Harboring expectations about how other people *should* act or treat you is usually a signal to look in the mirror. Getting upset that someone didn't show up or feeling that "they should've just known" can be an invitation to make the list of what you thought they should do, and then do those things for yourself. You may land on a whole new way of befriending yourself through this time.

Another potential outcome from writing this Dear Letter is that you may realize this particular friendship reveals a pattern of your friend's behavior. Not only were they not here for you *this* time, but they also weren't there for you at *other* times. This may indeed be a friendship you want to let go of. The Dear Letter will help you get clear about your hopes and expectations with this friendship so you'll know how to move forward.

A Dear Letter to Yourself

I am including a page called Dear Griever. You may choose to write a letter to yourself. Regardless of whether you chose to have a conversation with the other person, this is your opportunity to write all the things you wish you could've heard from them. The person in question may not have the ability to tell you what you want to hear. Can you do this for yourself? For example, I have developed a practice of being a good parent and friend to myself. Over the years, if I notice I am wishing a friend or parent would've done this or that for me,

I've empowered myself to do those things for *myself* so I'm not under the control of what someone else "should" have done. Read that again: I am no longer under that person's control. As I've let go of my expectations (and resentments) toward what others should be doing for me and taken responsibility for myself, I've freed myself from so much heartache. And so can you.

Try this. Below is a writing prompt. Please write a letter to yourself stating all the things you wish you would've heard or received from someone else, like this:

Dear Me,

I see this has been a hard time and you've gone through so much. I'm so sorry I wasn't there for you in the way you really needed me. I'm so proud of how far you've made it through this ordeal, and I want you to know you're doing great.

Sincerely,
Your Strength and Courage

Dear _____,

_____

_____

_____

Signed, _____

A Dear Letter to Your Person

A Dear Griever letter is also a signal to reach out to other trusted friends, let them know what it is I want or need, and ask if they're willing to be a part of helping me take care of me. You wouldn't believe how wildly well received this is when I articulate my wants and needs to those who care for me. Especially with my husband.

Most partners really want to make their beloved happy, but they don't always know how to do this, and trust me, people really can't read your mind. Darin and I have come to a place where I'm able to write a quick note or send a text about what I need (time together, a hug, a listening ear, dinner out), and he usually comes home ready and willing to meet that need. It gives him a guide and specific steps about how to help me. In this way, we both win. Rather than making him swim around in a world of guessing, seeing me upset, and trying to read my mind, this approach is like a road map to his wife. In turn, he offers me insight into his own needs, so I can show up and help the most important person in my life feel good. By doing this, we set ourselves up for success. And isn't that what we all want? Successful, satisfying relationships? Yes! Keep going. I want you to try this practice.

Next, write a letter to your closest person in life, and try asking for a bit of what you need right now, like this:

Dear My Person,

I'm feeling sad and could use a hug and a friend to watch a movie with tonight or this weekend. I could also use some encouragement as I'm

feeling low. Would you mind coming to mass with me next weekend? I
feel more hopeful in my faith setting. Also, I need ice cream!

Sincerely,
Your Person (Me)

—————————————————————

Dear ——————————,

—————————————————————————

—————————————————————————

—————————————————————————

Signed, ———————————————————

* * *

The Dear Letters can lead to truly close intimacy with your-self and perhaps with others. When you become vulnerable and let somebody know how you feel, you are allowing them to see inside of you. By having those crucial yet difficult conversations, it's quite possible to build an essential relationship that's warm, deeply connected, satisfying, and safe.

This is your opportunity to leave it all on the table. The next chapter will begin to build a new story, but we can't do that until you have clarity, have processed your grief, and understand the lesson to be learned. The wound must be fully debrided. I invite you to write as many letters as you need. If you're going through this book for the first time, there might be things from your past that you realize you've never addressed. You might have some time in this chapter to write multiple letters. I encourage you to do that work before moving to the next chapter.

Chapter 8

The New Story

"Grief is an alteration of who we once were, to who we become now. It's an adjustment of ourselves, an adaptation to our souls. We don't work through our grief and return to who we once were."

—KATHY PARKER, WRITER, POET

SANDY HOOK PROMISE

The Sandy Hook Elementary School shooting has the unfortunate distinction of being known as the deadliest mass shooting at an elementary school or high school in U.S. history so far.

And it's the only way I can ensure that no other parent feels the unrelenting pain of losing their child to gun violence. I know in my heart that we are preventing this from happening to other people and honoring my little

Daniel. We have already prevented school shootings. We have already prevented suicides, overall violence. We're bringing down bullying. So they don't have to be in my shoes. So they don't have to carry around pictures of their child.

These are the words of Sandy Hook parent-survivor Mark Barden and his wife Jackie, who have parlayed their unimaginable losses into a national movement to stop gun violence. Their organization is called the Sandy Hook Promise. Their son Daniel was a victim of the 2012 Newtown, Connecticut mass shooting that left twenty children between six and seven years old and six adult staff members dead.

Mark and Jackie have rallied millions of people through their grassroots organization in their efforts to educate and prevent violence against children. They've conducted research, established a nationwide hotline, and developed an app for safely reporting warning signs and potential threats if a classmate or teacher thinks a student may be at risk of becoming a shooter. They have created reform in our legal system and protected children in schools through their Volunteer Protection Program, which helps schools be prepared in the event that they are targeted for violence. At the writing of this book, Mark and his team have aired their educational programs to more than twelve million participants, and more than eighty million views of their back-to-school, public service safety announcement have occurred.

In 2010, when their son was only four years old, they were a normal family. Through horrendous circumstances, they have become leaders in a culture that has to reckon with the violence it allows. They've written a new story, not only for themselves and other Sandy Hook families but for government officials, law enforcement, everyday citizens, other survivors, the media, and millions of other people. In the years since the Sandy Hook mass shooting, more than twenty state legislatures have expanded background check requirements on some type of firearms. Some states have also passed red flag laws, which give law enforcement the power to confiscate weapons belonging to those who may pose a danger to themselves or others.

The Bardens experienced something called *post-traumatic growth*, which is the positive mental shifts that some people undergo as a result of facing great adversity and loss. Even though Mark and Jackie Barden would've never chosen or wanted this life, they've taken the very worst that life has offered them and transformed it into life-changing work on behalf of others. I'd like you to now consider what your *new story* is going to be.

REWRITING A NEW CHAPTER

As we begin to craft your new story in the wake of loss, this particular work is some of the most crucial you will do. As you begin to identify the takeaways, bottom lines, and new work life has in store for you, it's important to capture every part of it because there are many messages here for you. My hope while you work through this chapter is that you can experience your own resilience.

There are several ways to rewrite a new chapter for moving forward. What follows is a series of prompts and questions to help you begin thinking about your next steps and what this loss has taught you.

Are there ways that the loss you've been through has affected the direction of your life?

- Have you changed the focus of your work to be in more alignment with your struggles?

- Do you have a new perspective on life after your ordeal?

- Are you more drawn to people who have gone through what you have?

- Are you interested in making a difference in the community based on your grief and loss? Have you earmarked money or resources to help others endure what you've had to go through?

- Are you drawn to doing research in the areas of your loss?

- Are you interested in working to help bring resources to others like yourself or to their families?

- Have you had creative ideas about how to help those affected by their own loss? Like write a book, make a movie, create a song, open a business?

How, in the long run, do you imagine you'll give this loss meaning in your life?

Some people may find that keeping in touch with others they met through their experience keeps the meaning alive for them. Others allow their loss to fuel new changes in their lives. Still others find that finishing something their loved one wanted to accomplish but never did is very meaningful for them. I've also heard that some find significance in working to change the future so that others will not have to endure what they had to. This can take the form of setting up scholarships or foundations or changing legislation.

What are you doing differently now?

- As of today, what has changed for you?

- Do you have an increased awareness of any kind?

- Do you spend your time thinking differently?

- Have you made specific changes?

- Do you have new goals?

- Have you had important conversations or made any new decisions or promises because of your challenges?

Has anything good come of this loss, of this new life you're living that perhaps you didn't want to live?

- Do you have new energy for living?

- Have you discovered any "next steps" for yourself?

- Have you made needed changes?

- Are you willing to take responsibility and accept accountability for yourself in any new ways? (Note: this can have life-changing ramifications for yourself and those around you).

- Have you found your voice in a new way?

- Have you uncovered any new strengths, hobbies, or pastimes that you didn't know you had or could enjoy?

Have you found any insight, benefits, or gifts that came from your grieving? If so, what?

- Do you see yourself as a stronger person?

- Are others drawn to you now for your expertise and help?

- Have you experienced the clarifying process of loss, that once you lose someone or something, it cuts through noise of less important things and helps you focus on that which is more valuable?

- Are your relationships better?

- Do those around you feel more loved and valued by you?

What qualities in yourself have you drawn on that have contributed to your resilience?

Here are some examples:

- Access to a sense of courage you never knew you had

- Leaning into a community that bolstered you through these difficult times

- Deepening into your faith

- Utilizing exercise and physical movement in a way like never before

- Writing, drawing, or expressing yourself in new ways

How has your loss affected your sense of priorities?

Perhaps going through this difficult time has prompted you to reevaluate things such as where you live, your appearance, who you spend time with, what kind of job you do, or how you parent. Perhaps your loss has enabled you to examine your priorities, to decide what truly matters, and shed the things that don't.

What is most important to you now?

Include a few sentences here about what you want your life to look like and where you want to focus your time.

What lessons, if any, about loving and being close to others you care for has this loss taught you?

For instance, are you more likely to spend time with certain people in life? Are you more present and focused with the people that you care about?

Has this loss deepened your love or your gratitude for anyone or anything?

Are you more appreciative of your pet? Are you more appreciative of your children or perhaps have new love in your life? Has this amplified your love and appreciation for your neighbors?

How has this loss contributed to a new outlook on your life?

For instance, if you've overcome a traumatic and catastrophic illness, does just the fact that you can walk and talk and breathe feel exciting to you? If you've been able to heal your marriage after betrayal, are you able to savor the new depths of intimacy you and your spouse have discovered in the process?

Do you have any goals at this present time? Do you feel a burning desire to do something specific with your life?

Sometimes people who undergo tremendous tragedy feel more galvanized and more ready than ever to take on big life challenges. One person I know heard that her dying mother had an unfinished "Bucket List" and she promised herself that after her mother died, she would finish the list herself as a way to honor her mom.

What could you do if you were no longer grieving?

For instance, you may say things like the following:

- When I'm done grieving or when things don't feel so heavy, I can see myself traveling.

- I can see myself making a film.

- I can go back to school.

- I can mentor others.

Complete this sentence: "Although I am sad, I am still able to _____."

Even though we're in grief, there's also a time when we're out of grief, like an accordion.

Although I am sad, I am still able to tend my garden.

- Even though I am crying daily, I am still able to hug my children.

- Even though I am angry, I am still able to pet my dog.

- Although I am in shock, I am still able to say hello to my neighbors.

- Although I am in disbelief, I am still able to take a moment and pray for other people that were impacted by my loss as well.

Sometimes this helps us feel relief to know that grief, loss, sadness, and disbelief are not our only companions.

Can you begin to mobilize your own self-healing?

We tend to "think" before we do, even if it's just for a second. We will see ourselves *doing* a thing in our mind's eye before we *do it*. What can you see yourself doing right now that could help you? Taking a nap or a quiet stroll, having that conversation, writing that letter, or getting a facial? What pops into your mind as you think about self-healing?

Is it OK for you to be OK, at least for a while?

There are times when people who are going through loss feel guilty if they begin to feel better. They think if they move forward, accept what has happened, or take on new challenges, that it may appear they don't love or miss what they've lost. It is OK for you to work on healing yourself and still grieve and miss your loved one. The two can coexist.

Please complete this sentence: "The next thing I want to do is _____."

When you ask yourself this question, I want you to ask and then listen quietly for your inner wisdom to silently answer. This is a way to become attuned to yourself that you may have never known existed. If your response is that the next thing you want to do is *take a nap* or *go see a friend* or *help other families,* trust that instinct. That same inner wisdom may whisper something like *the next thing I want to do is go back to school so I can help other people.* If so, your inner light is guiding you. That's what happened to me.

When I think about the future, I think _____
_____.

Again, allow your heart to fill in this blank. Possible responses you might hear are

- "I think I'll be very sad, but I can still find the courage to go forward;"

- "My loved one would want me to do that;"

- "When I think about the future, I think there may be a second chance waiting for me;" or

- "When I think about the future, I think I may need to go talk to somebody who can support me."

What has changed for me?

Sit with that question for a while. We've done some exploration through previous chapters about things that have changed: rules in your head that you've amended, beliefs you've developed, lessons you've learned, feelings you have. All of that information can't help but transform you. Here is the time when you get to articulate what has changed for you.

An answer I've heard is, "What has changed for me is that I don't take anything for granted anymore. Life is very short, and we are not guaranteed tomorrow. And so today, I'm going to live as if this is my last day." If that has changed for you, and you've been riveted to the present moment like never before, write that down. On the other hand, if you now have a skepticism and fear about life, where you feel so jolted and untrusting, that your very existence—your very stability in this world—is in question, I want you to write that down. "What has changed for me is that I now feel fractured, and I don't know what to do." That's good information.

What am I thankful for right now?

This question helps you examine what you can feel grateful for. You may not feel you have anything to be grateful for. I understand that; nevertheless, I want you to try this practice. *I am thankful for* _____ *now*. Using the word *now* adds a sense of urgency. Most people can't help but interact with this phrase. I'm not just thankful, but I'm thankful *right now*, for my awareness, for the ability to write, for the house I live in, that I still have my family, or that I still have my job. Please name three things that you're thankful for *right now*.

What do my next steps look like?

If in some of the previous prompts you wrote, "I don't feel trusting about life. I feel very fractured. I'm quite upset. I don't see any point in living life," then your next steps might look like, "...and I want to talk to somebody about that," or, "I want to find relief from that, and so I will..." And this is where you get specific. "I will go see somebody I trust. I will see a physician, a therapist, a pastor, or a best friend."

* * *

For others, this may be the time when it's all coming together. You begin to look at what's next. What would it look like if you took the lessons learned, the changes you've made, the feelings you've been processing, and the experiences you've had and did something with them? If you're not sure what that is, let me ask you the miracle question: what does your ideal world look like? If you went to sleep tonight and woke up in the morning with a world that looked exactly how you wanted it to, what would that look like? Paint me a picture.

- How are you spending your time? For example, if you're helping other people going through the same loss or grief you experienced, how are you doing it?

- Who are you with? If you have the strongest and best relationships, what did you do to have those relationships?

- You have your dream job. What is that? How did you get there?

- Where do you live? How do you live?

This is the point where you deepen into figuring out your dream, what you'd like life to look like, and how you can get there. Now, what are one or two steps you can take in that direction? This is an important part of experiencing post-traumatic growth.

Exercise

Now complete these prompts for yourself:
- How has loss has affected the direction of your life?
- In the long run, how do you imagine you'll give this loss meaning in your life?
- What are you doing differently now?

- Has anything good come of this loss?
- Have you found any insight, benefits, or gifts that came from your grieving? If so, what?
- What qualities in yourself have you drawn on that have contributed to your resilience?
- How has your loss affected your sense of priorities?
- What is most important to you now?
- What lessons has this loss taught you, if any, about loving and being close to those you care for?
- Has this loss deepened your love or your gratitude for anyone or anything?
- How has this loss contributed to a new outlook on your life?
- Do you have any goals at the present time?
- What could you do if you were no longer grieving?
- "Although I am sad, I am still able to _____."
- Can you begin to mobilize your own self-healing?
- Is it OK for you to be OK, at least for a while?
- "The next thing I want to do is _____."
- "When I think about the future, I think _____."
- What has changed for you?
- What are you thankful for right now?
- What do your next steps look like?

BRINGING IT ALL TOGETHER—CREATING A PERSONAL STATEMENT

Answering these questions is the first part, but then you've got to get into action. Let's talk about how you do that.

Now we get to take all the nuggets of gold you've gotten from every other chapter and write it out into your own personal statement. This is your opportunity to synthesize it all so you can see the arc of your story.

- My Story that happened

- What I was feeling

- My experience

- What I lost

- My new beliefs

- My Essential *And* statements

- What I would do differently

- What I want to do now

Your answers should fill one or two pages and you can update them as you change. Your story is still being written, like a live journal or diary. And because life is hard, you'll return to these questions again and again as you face new loss. Answering these questions may provide a sense of increased positive emotion or relief of some of the negative ones. Do this with purpose and intent; it might suck in the moment, but you'll feel better after it's completed because these questions crystallize your story. Not only will you feel better but you'll also be prepared for the next step of naming your purpose.

RISING AGAIN

When I went through this process for myself, I realized that loss was preparing me to become a therapist, writer, and leader. I don't like that it happened this way, and yet I get to do this work now. I made meaning of my loss, and revealed my next step. The point of loss is where my life came together.

How has grief been good for me? Opening my own therapy practice, hosting grief retreats, and writing this book were the final steps in a long process of finally being able to use all my experiences to help other people. There's something there for you to discover as well that won't necessarily be immediately apparent. This chapter should bring it all together for you. I can't say when. It might not be today, and you might have to do some of these exercises more than once. You might have to revisit them. How you respond to the questions depends on how your grief evolves.

In *Man's Search for Meaning*, Viktor Frankl wrote about seeking a *happy life* versus seeking a *meaningful life*. One doesn't necessarily lead to the other.

Happy lives don't generally lead to meaningful lives all the time, and meaningful lives often don't produce happiness, but they do produce a lot of satisfaction.

The work he did in those concentration camps, followed by the profound work he did afterward as a survivor, was so powerful that it shaped the rest of his life. All the questions in this chapter were answered for Frankl even though he didn't want any of it. I have no doubt that your life right now and the loss you're experiencing is not how you wanted your life to be. All the Sandy Hook parents feel the same way. Frankl would've rather done anything else, but it led to his crowning work and brought him to his life's purpose.

Everything great I've ever done began with loss. Parenting was a loss of life without children; it was a loss of freedom and time. Experiencing a wonderful marriage came after the loss of my first marriage. Being in my career and helping people was a direct result of losing my health. Getting fired from a job brought clarity about who I wanted to be. All this to say that life is preparing you for something. It may be trying to tell you it's time to use your gifts. That very loss is moving you into your life's purpose. Grief is a change agent. Instead of being your undoing, that loss could be your making.

In the final chapter, I'll show you how to manage and move through your loss in the long term.

Chapter 9

Living With Honor
After Your Loss

"Barn's burnt down—now I can see the moon."

—MIZUTA MASAHIDE

TRANSFORMED:
POST-TRAUMATIC GROWTH

My friend Kayla was diagnosed with an aggressive form of breast cancer at just twenty-four years old. She survived the fiery trials of cancer treatment, radiation, the removal of both of her breasts, and dozens of medications. And now she faces a lifetime of follow-up care. By age thirty, she was still on chemotherapy, her entire body and life upended by an illness. Even after everything she's been through, she says she feels an excitement and zest for life that she never had before and finds deep satisfaction in her work. She's somehow savoring nearly every day. She's alive. She's produced an epic documentary about the young adult cancer experience that has been shown at Harvard Medical School and is currently streaming on Amazon. I wonder: *how does she do it?* Like the Bardens after Sandy Hook, she experienced post-traumatic growth.

When we go through the grieving process and meet it all the way, to the best of our ability, it can transform us.

We show up for the transformation process, but often we don't know what that means or what it will look like. Our culture is so busy valuing productivity and efficiency that often we end up going back to what we know, even though it's not good for us.

This chapter provides a framework to keep you moving forward now that you have some clarity about your grief and loss. There are specific micro-practices within the work of *When Grief Is Good* that will keep you in a state of processing and off-loading your hurts. I always feel like we're given light enough for the next step on our path. As you move beyond the acute grief that often accompanies the early stages of loss, it's not unusual to get stuck because you don't know what to do next. The checklist offers a way to check in with yourself and see the next point of light. It's meant to be a guide. If you want to be intentional about taking the life lessons from your loss so grief can be good for you, the checklist provides several ways to do that. I offer prompts to take care of yourself and remain open to the possibilities as you move into the next steps and into your future.

The best approach is to first read through checklist and pick one item that stands out the most, seems the most doable, or has the most positive energy around it.

LIVING WITH HONOR—MICRO-GRIEVING CHECKLIST

❑ I reached out to family, friends, elders, or colleagues for comfort and companionship but gave myself permission to back off when I needed time alone.

❑ I took the initiative to reach out to folks from whom I might not normally seek help.

❑ I looked for new friends in church groups, social groups, work, or school, or I went on the internet to find others who experienced a similar loss. I made a list of these supports to turn to when I was struggling or experiencing pain.

❑ I forced myself to be with people and to do things, even when I didn't feel like it, so I could stop isolating myself. I allowed myself to tell people how much I loved, admired, and cared for them.

❑ I hugged and held others but felt free to tell people when I did not want to be touched.

❑ I learned to grieve and mourn in public.

❏ I shared my story with others who I thought would appreciate and benefit from it.

❏ I told safe people the story of the deceased, even if they had nothing to say back.

❏ I gave and received random acts of kindness.

❏ I connected with animals and nature, for example, the deceased's pet, a beautiful sunset, a nature trail, or a garden.

❏ I cared for or nurtured others. For example, I spent time caring for my loved ones or children.

❏ I found my faith or religion comforting. I participated in religious, cultural, or ethnic mourning practices, such as attending church services, sitting shiva, participating in a wake, celebrating the Day of the Dead, visiting a memorial shrine, etc.

❏ I sought help from organized bereavement groups, hospices, religious groups, grief retreats, talking circles, or groups specific to the way the deceased died, such as cancer or violent loss like suicide or homicide.

❏ I sought help from mental health professionals. For instance, I attended counseling sessions or took medications as advised by my providers.

❏ I read books written by others who have coped with the loss of a loved one or been through a storyline like mine.

❏ I examined the thoughts and feelings that kept me from taking care of myself physically and emotionally, such as guilt, shame, sense of lost self, and loss of the will to live.

❏ I established routines of daily living. Although things were different, I made new routines and did not berate myself when I was not "perfect."

❏ I maintained personal hygiene, medical care, healthy nutrition, and regular sleep.

❏ I reconnected with my body through exercise, yoga, Tai Chi, or expressive arts, allowing myself time to get stronger.

❏ I recognized that my brain needed time to heal and for things to improve, so I forgave myself when I made mistakes, became distracted, couldn't remember, or didn't understand.

❏ I avoided the excessive use of alcohol, tobacco, recreational drugs, and caffeine as a coping mechanism.

❏ I relinquished avoidance and learned to face my fears by engaging in life. I participated in activities that had meaning and kept me occupied, such as work, hobbies, crafts, singing, or dancing.

❏ I allowed myself to pursue and feel positive emotions, such as compassion toward myself and others, expressions of gratitude, and emotions of love, joy, awe, and hopefulness.

❏ I recognized and labeled my feelings, viewing them as a "message" rather than something to avoid. I accepted and dealt with these emotions, understanding that the less I fought them, the more I was able to handle them.

❏ I regulated my strong negative emotions using slow, smooth breathing, coping self-statements, prayer, or other mood-regulating techniques.

❏ I allowed myself time to cry and gave words to my emotional pain.

❏ I distinguished feelings of grief from other feelings such as fear, uncertainty, guilt, shame, and anger.

❏ I expressed difficult feelings through writing and talking to supportive others.

❏ I used journaling, reflective writing, letter or poetry writing, or other expressive arts such as scrapbooking, dance, or music.

❏ I engaged in gratitude activities, telling others how much I appreciate their love and support, reminding myself of the things that I am thankful for, and being grateful that I knew the deceased.

❏ I established a safe and comforting space for myself, either physically or through imagery.

❏ I stayed connected to the deceased and created a new relationship, while recognizing the reality of the loss.

❏ I attended a group to help me move through my story of loss (divorce care, etc.)

❏ I examined the feelings and thoughts that kept me from forming an enduring connection with the deceased, such as the fear of what others would think of me, guilt, shame, humiliation, disgust, or thoughts of anger, revenge, or preoccupation with my grief.

❏ I participated in practices such as visiting the grave or memorial site, celebrating special occasions, prayer and candlelight vigils, public memorials, or commemorative services.

❏ I commemorated the deceased's life with words, pictures, or things, or created a small place of honor for the deceased that I could visit any time I chose.

❏ I thought about what I received from the deceased and the legacy and mission to be fulfilled.

❏ I became involved in a cause or social action that was important to the deceased or myself.

❏ I created a legacy by planting a tree, starting a scholarship or charity in the deceased's name, starting an internet blog, or launching new family or community practices.

❏ I allowed myself to talk to the deceased and allowed myself to listen.

❏ I wrote a letter to my loved one and asked for advice.

❏ I asked for forgiveness, shared joys and sorrows, and constructed a farewell message.

❏ I accepted that sadness was normal and learned how to be with my grief.

❏ I learned how to contain my grief to a time and place of my choosing. However, I understood that intense upsurges of grief may arise unexpectedly and without warning, and I developed coping strategies to handle such events.

❏ I used imagery, shared stories, and photos of my loved one, or purposefully used reminders such as music or special routines, to recall positive memories.

❏ I cherished and hung on to specific, meaningful possessions (objects, pets, etc.).

❏ I actively reminisced, holding on to our relationship in my heart and mind.

❏ I reached out to help and support others who are grieving for their loved ones. Helping others is a way to reengage in life and combat loneliness and tendencies to withdraw and avoid social contacts.

❏ I examined the thoughts that fuel my fears, avoidance, and the belief that I cannot or should not feel happy and that things would never get better.

❏ I took a breather and gave myself permission to rest, knowing that grieving takes time and patience, with no quick fixes.

❏ I identified memories that trigger or overwhelm me and disengaged and/or established boundaries by limiting people, places, or things that cause me stress or overwhelm me so that I could address them one by one, in my own time.

❏ I learned to say no to unreasonable requests.

❏ I identified important activities, places, or things that I was avoiding due to fear of my grief reactions. I slowly reintroduced them or allowed myself to choose the ones I never wanted to encounter again.

❏ I began to think of myself as a "survivor" if not a "thriver" of my own story rather than as a "victim."

❏ I reminded myself of my strengths and of all the hard times I've gotten through in the past.

❏ I wrote out reminders of how to cope and put them on my fridge, cell phone, or computer. I looked at them when I was struggling and reminded myself of ways to be resilient.

❏ I created a plan for how to cope with difficult times.

❏ I learned to anticipate and recognize potential "hot spots" of when things are most difficult. I rated each day on a scale of one to ten on how well I was doing. I asked myself what I could do to make things better and increase my rating.

❏ I worked on increasing the number of good days compared to the number of bad days.

❏ I avoided thinking *this is just how it is,* realizing that I have choices no matter how hard life is.

❏ I came to recognize that emotional pain can be a way to stay connected with my loved one and asked myself if there were other ways to stay connected that didn't hurt so much.

❏ When I was overwhelmed by negative memories of the past, I avoided "time-sliding" into the past.

❏ I "grounded" myself to the present by refocusing my attention on the environment around me.

❏ I changed my self-talk by telling myself *I am safe* and that *this will pass.*

❏ I controlled my bodily reactions by slowing down my breathing.

❏ I oriented to people's faces, voices, or touch, or called for help from a friend.

❏ I moved toward a future outlook and a stronger sense of self.

❏ I examined the false thoughts and feelings that kept me from moving forward, such as I am dishonoring the deceased by getting better, I am leaving him/her behind, feeling happier means that he/she is no longer important to me, or that my love for him/her is fading.

❏ I regained my sense of hope for the future. I worked to reestablish a sense of purpose with meaningful short-, mid-, and long-term goals.

❏ I am creating a life worth living, taking control of my future.

❏ I worked on regaining my sense of self-identity, knowing that my life had changed, but that I am still me.

❏ I focused on what is most important for this day only.

❏ I developed new goals and action plans, consistent with what I value.

❏ I created purpose by keeping the memory of the deceased alive in others.

❏ I kept others aware of the circumstances of the death so that some good could come from the loss.

❏ I transformed my grief and emotional pain into mean-ing-making activities that created something "good and helpful." Examples include Mothers Against Drunk Driving and the Melissa Institute for Violence Prevention.

❏ I use my faith-based and religious or spiritual beliefs to comfort me and move on. This includes scripture, sacred writings, a connection to God, and my beliefs about life and my loved one such as *my loved one can continue to influence the lives of others in the world, my loved one is no longer suffering and is in a safe place,* or *we will be reunited in the future.*

For a complete list of the Micro-Grieving Checklist, please visit https://www.cindyfinch.com/.

DAILY PRACTICE OF MICRO-GRIEVING

Grief doesn't become good for us unless we take a role in it. The daily practice of micro-grieving means regularly doing one or multiple items on this list to release the buildup of grief, like a pressure valve; this is how we can begin to feel better. Doing something on a daily or regular basis, in a safe space, keeps it from becoming overwhelming. Use any one of these when you are in distress or a negative state around your grief, to help move yourself out of it. But this is not the only time; the hope is that you onboard the practice of this list as a new, regular way of life.

Conclusion

I have faced down some terrible things in my life. I've had doctors make mistakes that almost killed me; I've been in the ICU of the world's scariest hospitals. I've had traumatic surgeries and procedures performed on me under emergency conditions. People less sick than me have died right next to me. And if I'm still alive, there must be a reason. I want to use the life I've been given as a way to help others.

I let the losses teach me what they needed to teach me. Even if I was thrown under the wave, I learned how to stand up, to recover over and over again, and to survive. I pulled from my faith and my grit, and in the middle of all of it, a soul grew. It made me strong. I began to thrive. I developed an immense capacity to endure hard times. I understood suffering (as much as a white, middle-aged American woman can understand suffering). Suffering became a companion and a teacher. I learned a lot about myself and the world, about my family, my faith, my priorities, and my values. After everything I experienced, I realized that other people experienced similar loss, heartbreak, and dysfunction, with no effective coping mechanisms. I wanted to help.

A POINT OF LIGHT ON THE PATH

One of the things I lacked throughout much of my life was access to other, more experienced people to guide me through my loss. My husband and I didn't know a soul who had ever been through experiences like ours. So, when I came through to the other side of my loss, I wanted to be that for other people. For you. I made it my mission to be for others the resource that hadn't existed for me. I would be a point of light on their path in whatever way I could.

I started in a grassroots manner around the community, through outreach. I first connected with cancer patients by writing letters. Then I began speaking at gatherings and events. I visited cancer patients in the hospital and corresponded with their families, especially young survivors and patients. I developed programs at the Gift of Life Transplant House for isolated heart and lung patients that had been pushed into the back alleys of the medical world. I became proactive in the community because I was determined to give other people what I had lacked. My writings have made it all over the world, and it feels like all of this is what I was meant to do with the second chance I've been given.

I began meeting people for coffee. I helped them with their problems, encouraged them in their faith through difficult times, and helped them lean into the life lessons that challenged them. "Hey, the next time you go for coffee with somebody, why don't you swipe a credit card?" my husband said one day. "You're doing this so often that it's become like a profession," he quipped. "And when you're not meeting with people, you're creating programs, launching conferences, and making content."

Eventually, my outreach and efforts led me back to grad school. I got my master's degree and opened a counseling practice. My practice was a natural outgrowth of the energy that inspired me to help others after the worst part of my difficulties were over. And not just when they were over, but when I learned how to move with them and through them. I filtered down my work very specifically to serve a community of people who were fielding core-shaking events that the average person wouldn't know how to grapple with: traumatic illness or the unexpected death of a loved one. I was comfortable dealing with big things like murder, suicide, traumatic loss, and complicated storylines of life jumping the tracks. Bittersweetly, I am quite at home in the depths of human loss and grief. If it's big and tragic, it has my name on it.

What I learned is that grief and loss are the doorway to greatness, the doorway to activate our gifts through loss. I realized that all my past grief and loss carved out this space in my soul for helping others through their worst times. And that was the springboard that led me to the work I do today. By now, I've worked with thousands of people across the country on all kinds of platforms. That path has continued to shine a light for me. The fuel I use now to do the hard work of a good marriage and a good life has come from prolific failure. Today, my work provides lessons that equip me as a therapist like no grad school, training, or PhD ever could.

IT'S TIME TO USE YOUR GIFTS

There is so much nobility in your grief. You are the caterpillar who thought the world was over, but it was going into the cocoon, not to die but to transform. Death for the caterpillar is transformation and birth for the butterfly. I hope this book supports you in discovering ways to move out of grief, to understand your purpose in this world and where to go from here.

If you're ready to let grief be your guru and continue to move with and through your loss, find me at my website: https://www.cindyfinch.com.

The next steps in healing will look different for everyone. Maybe you're interested in an online class or a retreat. Maybe you'd like to give this book to your therapist. Maybe you'd like to have a family member read it. Whatever you do, I hope you find power, inspiration, and healing in your journey.

Appendix

ON THAT SHORE

Micro-Grieving Practice

Poem by Cindy Finch

*If I should go and skies turn gray
and life swings long and low,*

*If clouds should burst and hearts should break
and between us time should grow*

*Then know that I've but morphed a bit
and flown on up ahead,*

*To wait upon the shores of God on this path
that I've been led.*

WHEN GRIEF IS GOOD

*I'll sing, I'll dance, I'll play all day
and the stories I will hear,*

*From those who've gone before me,
and from those who now are near.*

*Rumors and longings from this secret place
have billowed through my mind,*

*Years I've longed to see my home
and now at last it's time.*

Time for songs, time for joy, time for walks and talks,

*Time to know as I've been known
as mysteries are unlocked.*

*My heart will bloom, His glory full,
my Lover now revealed!*

My feet upon His grass and my cartwheels in His fields.

*My hero and I will laugh and sing,
His nobles I will greet,*

*They've butterflied away like I, now His grass
beneath their feet.*

*Long and sweet I'll drink it in,
this new life from my old,*

But know each day the shores I'll walk as I've grown
now young from old.

Know that I am waiting and longing for that time

When your steps will meet my shore again

And your hand joins back in mine.

I'll leap, I'll run, I'll chase you down,

I'll kiss you high and low!

I'll tuck, I'll hug, I'll sweep you up

There upon that shore.

Your nose and ears I'll bite and chew
as if they were a cake!

My heaven will expand then,
when you, upon that shore I take.

When dance and laughs and sweet relief's
give full sail to this "Us"

We'll talk, we'll tell of our sweet paths
that heaven's brought us to discuss.

I'll tell of times when from His lap,
your face, your life I poured

WHEN GRIEF IS GOOD

The fragrant wine of our dear love
and my longings from that shore.

My Captain how He'd silk my hair
and gently touch my face

His hands, his love will silk you too,
as we wait for our embrace.

So dawn with me, step high and light
when life pulls hard and mean

I've butterflied, the days will fly,
'til I greet you on that beach.

My kiss, my hugs will wait for you
and then still all the more,

When in that time, my God
and I will meet you on that shore.

—2006

Collateral Losses Table

TYPE OF LOSS	LOSS OF...
Divorce	Security and predictability
	Partnership
	Two parents in the same house
	Financial stability
	Status
	Ex-partner's family and friends
	Shared events and traditions
	Family trips
	Time with kids because of shared custody
	Shared history and memories
	A best friend
	Special places once shared together
	Other person in the same bed/comfort and closeness
	Self-confidence
	Trust in life, God, and others
	Sense of control over the family

TYPE OF LOSS	LOSS OF...
Leaving or Losing a Job	**Financial security**
	Sense of identity and worth
	Daily schedule
	Status
	Sense of purpose
	Sense of safety
	Belief in the good of others (when let go)
	Relationships with coworkers
	Self-confidence
	Future plans/retirement
Loss of Pet	**Partnership**
	Friendship
	Daily comfort
	Play partner
	Family member
	Sense of losing one's child
	Reasons to get out of the house and go for a walk
	Motivation

Collateral Losses Table

TYPE OF LOSS	LOSS OF...
Loss of Health/Health Challenges	Identity
	Energy
	Freedom
	Youth
	Independence
	Simple things
	Predictable future
	Structure
	A certain lifestyle
	Mobility
	Certainty
	Ableism
Betrayal by a Spouse	Faith in your "person"
	Sense of "knowing"
	Sense of safety
	Structure and predictability
	Friends and family
	Peace of mind
	Faith and beliefs in love and marriage
	The entire first marriage

TYPE OF LOSS	LOSS OF...
Pandemic and World Events	Health
	Loved ones
	Safe housing
	Other people's faces and smiles (community)
	Job, business, livelihood
	Milestones and celebrations (weddings, graduations, etc.)
	Independence and freedom
	Routine
	Friendships at work and school
	Safety
	Control
	Mental health
	Trust in national leaders

Acknowledgments

It is essential that I acknowledge certain people in my life who helped (i.e., *insisted*) that I write this book. First, my husband Darin. The assistance, support, encouragement, and feedback you gave me through this process is indescribable. You brought me plates of food as I sat behind my computer, helped me think through the larger concepts, and held me as I sat fractured and gutted by the stories that fill this book. Thank you for remembering *who I was* all those years ago and for your tireless care of me through the years, both as a patient and as your partner. Thank you for agreeing to be inside the rubber band with me, the one that brings us back to each other over and over again.

Thank you to our kids, Jordan, Zach, and Brandon. You three have cheered me on, mulled over ideas, and walked alongside me in ways a mom could never have dreamed. I am so thankful and proud to be your mom.

I'd also like to say thank you to Lori Jean Glass for "seeing me" on that September afternoon at the Glass House as we lined the walls with huge post-it notes. Thank you for the title of this book, and for hammering out a mind-map with me.

Without you, I would've avoided the full-frontal topic of grief in every way possible. Instead, you challenged me to "make grief good for us, Cindy, will you?" I will keep trying to do that. Thanks for encouraging me to host my first Darkness to Light Grief Intensive and walking with me while this all took shape.

Thanks to my extended Finch family for keeping our dog Bella on long afternoons of writing so I could have some peace and quiet. Her sweet antics were more enjoyed at your house than mine when I really needed to focus. Thanks also for your loving encouragement of me as a writer, not just with this book but with all of my articles you clipped out, called me about, and saved. Writers need some reviewers in their corner who are willing to put their art on the refrigerator door from time to time, with pride. Thanks for being proud of me.

To my clients and colleagues, thank you for teaching me so much about grief, loss, resilience, rising through the ashes, and walking through the dark nights of a soul. I'm speechless about what you have endured. I'm so honored you've allowed me to walk alongside you on this path.

Thanks also to the Kreeger side of my family for being willing to walk and talk with me through the losses my family has endured. Your kind attention and support is so appreciated. Cancer came out of nowhere, and you stood with us and our kids in so many ways. Mom, thanks for all your care through the years. Karen, thank you especially for reviewing my choppy fits and starts at writing this book. I appreciate your trained and loving eye. Kim and Chris, I love you.

Thanks to the Mennonite community of Rochester for taking us under your wing in our time of need. Mary and everyone else, thank you for your wonderful food, lovely singing, and steadfast care while we were away from our family.

Neighbors, youth pastors, grandparents, family members, friends, and even other cancer patients, you became a symphony of help around us. The song of help you sang around us is one of the main reasons I can write this book. Thank you to all of you who "protected" us through such hard times.

To Margie, the nurse who held me close in the cardiac care unit and taught me the importance of a good, cheap laugh and then called to check up on me when I got home: Thank you. I have modeled the care of my patients after you ever since we met.

Thanks to my mother-in-law Chris who came to visit for a weekend and wound up staying for nine months to help us! And thanks to my parents for their tireless efforts of caring for me and our young family during cancer and beyond.

In my heart, I carry these names—the ones who are no longer here, the ones who taught me with their deaths—how to talk about and to be with loss. Some a little and some a lot. But all have pulled me along and moved this work forward. How can I ever thank you for all that you taught me, long after you knew you did? Keith, Jack, Dad, Colin, Sara, Vanessa, Kay, Kim, Sarah, Emma, Maiya, and Rick, thank you for your applause. Lee and Sharon, soldier on. We are with you.

Finally, I want to acknowledge God. For all the many sides of your mystery you've shown me, I know there are a million more to go. Thank you for cancer and all the other dark things. You know I never would've chosen it but would also never change it. "Once the barn burned down, I could finally see the moon."

PS: Amy, had you found the therapist you were looking for, I don't think any of this would've happened! Nomie and I are so grateful for you.

About the Author

Cindy Finch is a Licensed Clinical Social Worker (LCSW). Since completing her master's degree in Clinical Social Work and her training at Mayo Clinic, she has developed specialties in parenting today's teens and young adults, post-trauma growth, Dialectical Behavioral Therapy, complex-high-need-family interventions, traumatic loss and grief work for sudden death, and the management of a life-altering illness, all for the benefit of her clients.

Since 2013, she has authored and published works that have appeared on national websites and in publications like the *Los Angeles Times, HuffPost, CURE magazine, St. Anthony's Press, Chasing the Cure, Rochester Women's Magazine,* and more.

Cindy believes she can only take her clients as far as she has gone herself, so she has stayed active in her own personal growth and discovery. Her favorite way to grow is through new projects. Here are a few special projects she is intimately involved with right now:

***Vincible*:** a documentary film about young adults with cancer.

The Glass House: an intensive five-day retreat for those with deep relationship wounds and big life stories.

Pivot: a community working to transform relationships. Find out more at www.lovetopivot.com.

When she's not working, Cindy loves spending time with her family and being active with friends. She loves taking their pup Bella to Huntington Dog Beach, hiking all the great trails in Orange County, reading a good book, hugging her family, and trying new restaurants with her husband, Darin.